The Good Will Son

David S. Libbey

First Printing: 2019

ISBN 978-1-98433-295-0

David S. Libbey

28621 Brookhill Road
Trabuco Canyon, California 92679
dslibbey49@gmail.com

Dedication

This book is dedicated to my fallen friends
– Army and Marine Corps

Preface

I never intended to write a memoir — or any book for that matter. Like a lot of things in my life — it just happened. It started with a very short story — comments actually — on Facebook. Before I knew it, the comments from those first few paragraphs propelled me into writing short stories. The stories in this book are drawn from my life experiences. Each story was written to stand alone. However, when pieced together, they tell the story of a life — my life. I have tried to keep these stories as true to the facts as possible. Along the way, readers have helped refresh — and at times — correct my recollection of how things happened. For the most part, it has been a lot of fun. However, there are some stories here that were not so easy to write. At times, I found myself depressed for days after, or during, the writing process. But, I think it has been good therapy for me and for a few of my readers who lived through the events.

I've tried to add some humor in this memoir as well. At the end, I've written several chapters that are intended to be satirical. The Wine Cellar stories are based on real people. I have taken the liberty of exaggerating the characters and putting them in my fantasy world. I enjoy writing satire. I think I'll pursue that in my next efforts.

CHAPTER 1

Dad

Ifollowed him through the bowels of the cellar where he had taken a custodial job after his eyesight gave out. He lived in an apartment with my mother and maternal-grandmother on the top floor of a big white house on Cottage Road in South Portland, Maine.

To me, Hobbs Funeral Home seemed to be an odd and eerie place for him to end his working life. It didn't seem to bother him though. Death was nothing new to him. He had seen lots of it, and he had already come to terms with his own passing. The thought of dying no longer bothered him. Pointing to a plain, unfinished, pine-box stacked in the basement, he told me, "That's what I want to be buried in." I knew he meant it. The box was elegant in its simplicity. The artist in him would much rather that we saw the wood's swirling patterns of grain rather than have them covered. The casket's rope handles were functional and practical. He was a practical man. I'm sure he thought, "Why waste money on something that was going in the ground?"

When I think of him, I always picture him in his high-back rocking chair. If you left him alone, he would sit there for hours without saying a word. He always seemed to be far away — lost in thought — staring at something a thousand miles away. I often wondered what he could have been thinking about — rocking in his chair with that blank, unfocused gaze. I imagine there were a lot of things running through his mind before he passed. It wasn't until he was gone for many years that I thought I had begun to understand.

About ten years after he died, Mom gave me his military documents and his travel log. I guess she figured that having also been in the Marines, I would appreciate them more than anyone else. After reading his papers and looking at Mom's collection of photos, I began to see him differently. Mostly, I saw it in his eyes. I could see the changes taking place there in the old photographs — the photos taken before and then after the war — his war, not mine. His eyes had lost their brightness and had become those of an old, battle-weary soldier — one who had seen too much.

Now, don't get me wrong. He wasn't the stereotypical former Marine with PTSD — the kind they portray in the movies — the soldier who becomes sullen, violent or inconsolable. No, he was exactly the opposite in temperament. To be honest, I don't think I remember him ever raising his voice. Hell, it would hurt him more than me when it came time for discipline. He left that task to Mom. He was without a doubt the kindest and gentlest man I have ever known. He had a great sense of humor and a lot of patience — and believe me — I tested it.

Growing up, he had lived in a home for disadvantaged children for eight years — the Good Will Home in Hinckley, Maine. Sent there by his mother after his father died, it was there that he met and fell in love with another child of a single mother — Dorothea Briggs.

Maybe as he rocked in that chair, he imagined himself to still be on Guadalcanal, New Britain or on Peleliu with the 1st Marine Division. That was some of the most horrific fighting of the war in the Pacific. Maybe it was on one of those tiny islands that he saw too much — learned too much about man's inhumanity to man. We'll never know — he never spoke a word about it. But, it was there that he developed the malaria that plagued him for years after — it made him nauseous, gave him headaches and caused his skin to turn yellow. He carried that complexion for the rest of his life.

After the war, he went back to Maine and found "Dottie." By that time, she was a nurse working at the Maine General Hospital in Portland. Lucky for me and my siblings, Peter and Audrey, that he did find her. Otherwise, we wouldn't be here — the sons and daughter of two alumni of the Good Will-Hinckley Home.

Perhaps he just liked to rock and dream of his college days at Indiana Technical College. He had used the GI Bill to study engineering, and that's where I was born. After graduation, he, Mom, Peter and I moved back to Maine. We lived in a barn in the woods near South Portland High School with Mom's relatives. We lived with the sheep and chickens, while my step-grandfather built his home on Highland Avenue. Later, we moved into government housing for several years before he could afford the cottage at Willard Beach on Simonton Cove. He may have regretted putting all of his savings and sweat equity into that cottage for all those years only to have the city destroy it by undermining its foundation. When the city put that sewage treatment station next door, the house cracked open like an egg. They never apologized or took responsibility. Everything he had worked for was gone. His heart was broken.

Maybe he just felt comfortable rocking. Dad certainly deserved the rest and relaxation. He had worked as a draftsman at Bancroft and Martin and E. C. Jordan for most of his adult life. At night he mopped floors and cleaned toilets in downtown Portland to put Pete through college and medical school. If I had shown the aptitude or ambition, I'm sure he would have done the same for me. I know I didn't help matters by volunteering for the draft and heading off to Vietnam. After all, he had just lost his brother, Malcolm, in that war two months before I left for the Army.

Albert D. Libbey Jr. was a religious man — a Baptist. He liked teaching Sunday school and working with young people. Maybe instead of drinking, rocking was his way of self - medicating. When he and Mom married, they made a pact never to touch alcohol. You see, both of their fathers had died from it. So, they never touched a drop. Eventually, they completed their life-circle by taking on the job of house parents at Opportunity Farm — a home for disadvantaged children — they were back where they started. In the end, the cancer eventually took his life. He let it go untreated for too long.

If there is one regret in my life, it's that I didn't get to know him better or say good-bye. Perhaps then I would know the answers.

CHAPTER 2

Mom

She's blind now — well, not completely. She can still read the Bible with a magnifying glass. She can make her way around, but she can no longer see faces clearly. She knows people by their voices. Her hearing is not so good. She can no longer follow conversations in noisy places. The background noises interfere, and the strain of trying to listen tires her. She feels more comfortable in her retirement home. Her mind is clear; and her recall is remarkably good for someone who is ninety-five. She follows the news and is up to speed on current events. She sometimes wishes she wasn't up to speed, though. She thinks the world has gone mad. She longs for the simpler times — those days between her childhood and old age. She misses my dad and her church friends. Dad has been gone for twenty-four years. Those few friends who are still alive are either sick or have moved far away to be closer to their families. She misses her mother. Oh, how she misses her mother.

Grammy had to give her up when Mom's father died. His dying was a godsend and a curse. A godsend because she no longer had to hide when he came home drunk. She no longer had to fight off his unwanted advances. She no longer had to listen to him beating her mother. It was a curse, because she watched him die an alcoholic' death. It wasn't pretty. It was a slow death, one she can't forget. What she can't remember is what it felt like just to be a child. She never knew that feeling. When he was gone, she was sad and happy at the same time. You don't stop loving someone just because they mistreated you. But, she no longer had to hide or lock her bedroom door. For a short time, she could just be a little girl.

When Mom's father died, Grammy couldn't make it with two kids. She tried. She tried everything. She worked as a maid. She washed dishes in a restaurant. She took in laundry and watched the neighbor's children. It wasn't enough, though. The State of Maine gave her an ultimatum of choosing a home or having the State do it for her. Fortunately, she made a good choice.

The Good Will Home in Hinckley, Maine was as nice as could be expected. Mom received a good education there. Yes, it was a strict environment, but she was safe there. She didn't have to sleep behind a locked door. It was there that she met Dad. He was four years older and had been at Hinckley for five years. He courted her when he could. It wasn't easy. The girls were isolated from the boys. But, Dad found a way. After five years, you learn what you can and can't get away with in a place like that. Love always finds a way.

When Dad left the home and joined the Marine Corps, it was just before the Japanese attack on Pearl Harbor. He was gone for four years. Mom dated other boys and nearly married one. But when Dad returned, he came calling and she had to make a choice. I think she made the right one. Otherwise, I wouldn't be here. Mom became a nurse and worked at the Maine General Hospital in Portland. My parents had three kids — my older brother, Norman Peter, and my younger sister, Audrey.

Mom got religion after her father died. Growing up, we had family prayer meetings several times a week. We went to Sunday school and church twice on Sunday. We went to young peoples' meetings and Vacation Bible School. We went to religious camps in the summer, and religious retreats in the winter. We memorized the books of the Bible and certain verses that were important to Baptists. We were baptized and had to give our testimony in front of the congregation. Personally, I thought it was all a crock. But, that's not something you tell your parents.

Up until I began grade school, Mom and I were close — really close. She combed my hair, brushed my teeth and gave me baths. However, when I started school, I proved to be a poor student. I lacked focus. I couldn't sit still. Teachers said that I was easily distracted and was working well below my potential. Mom's love turned to disappointment. I remember that disappointment when I came home with a C on a third-grade paper. It wasn't good enough. She wanted me to be an A student. She had big dreams for me. She wanted me to become a doctor or lawyer. She wanted me to play an instrument — she tried to get me to play the piano, the accordion and the trombone. I wouldn't practice. I lacked the desire, and I longed to be outside playing with the other kids.

As I grew older and moved into my teenage years, I rebelled. I smoked, stayed out beyond curfew and became evasive about my whereabouts. Her disappointment turned to distrust. She went through my things looking for evidence of the things she knew I was concealing. She accused me of lying. She accused me of stealing. Sometimes I did. I continued to perform poorly in school, and when I became interested in girls, her distrust turned to dislike and disgust. I was a dirty boy. She was no longer proud to have me as her son. It wasn't long before locking me in the closet wasn't enough punishment. She turned to violence. I felt the sting of the belt, and at times, the pain from the buckle end. It went on like that until dislike turned into hatred, and hatred turned to madness. When she angered, a monster appeared. She would beat me in a frenzy with the buckle end of the belt, while foaming at the mouth like a mad dog. When I resisted, she threw me out of the house. I lived on the street, until weeks later my uncle and step-grandfather found me walking the streets of Portland. I lived with my grandmother for a long time. When Mom and Dad brought me back home, I stayed until after high school graduation. But it was never the same. I volunteered for the draft within six months. I couldn't stand living in that house. I was a sinner. I couldn't live up to her expectations. Vietnam couldn't be any worse.

I'm conflicted now. At sixty-nine, I still have mixed feelings. Although we reconciled, things will never be the same. You can never really repair a relationship once love becomes conditional. You can forgive, but you can never really forget. I see her once a year when I go to Maine. We talk weekly on the phone. But, it's strained. She's still trying to save my soul; but I'm beyond redemption. It's as if there's a big elephant in the room that we don't talk about.

She will never see this memory. When the time comes, I'll carry out her wishes. I'll stand before those who knew her and talk of our better days. As I said before, "You don't stop loving someone just because they mistreated you."

CHAPTER 3

Uncle Dana

"What'd I say, Dave? What'd I say?" He said that every time I saw him. It wasn't a follow-up to something he said. It had no special meaning — it was just his way of getting a rise out of me. It was silly, but it always made me laugh. Uncle Dana loved to laugh. He was a character. Dana was my dad's oldest younger brother. Dad had a lot of brothers and sisters — six brothers and four sisters from various marriages and liaisons. Uncle Dana was my favorite — perhaps because I knew him better than the rest. Dana was a cabinetmaker. He always had wood chips and sawdust in his coal black hair and on his arms. He was also a master carver with a lot of other talents. He carved musical instruments — violins and guitars. He was a self-taught classical guitarist. He was so good, that he was given the opportunity to play at Carnegie hall. It must have been difficult playing guitar while missing the little finger on his right hand. The finger was a casualty of his woodworking. He played the guitar for me right up until the medication for his cancer made it too hard for him to concentrate. He would stop in the middle of a song — close his eyes and drift off for a minute or two until he could get his composure back. I really think he was a genius. There was a lot of talent in the Libbey family back then. Every one of them did something special. We lost Dana at fifty-eight. All of the Libbey men seemed to die young.

When I was a kid, I would occasionally get to spend time with Uncle Dana. He would pick me up at the house at Willard Beach and drive us to his home in Rockland. We drove in his old Chevrolet jalopy that backfired. Every time it backfired, he would pretend he was firing a pistol with his hand. He would point out the window and pull his thumb back — the car would backfire — and he pulled his hand with the pointed index finder back from the recoil — we laughed all the way to Rockland. There were always a lot of people — relatives in the house in Rockland. There were always music stands, guitars and violins lying around. All of the Libbey men played an instrument or two. My grandfather, Albert Libbey Senior, was a traveling minstrel who played the banjo. I guess he passed his musical talents to his sons. There was also a chess board sitting in the parlor. The Libbey men would sit for hours playing chess and smoking their pipes. I loved the smell of that cherry tobacco.

When I was in my teens, Dana moved to Gray, Maine. Uncle Dana's family lived in the country in Gray. Their house was on a hill overlooking acres of farm land. The house was modest — unfinished. A Billy-goat guarded the well in the front yard. The outhouse was on the opposite side of the dirt driveway from the house. Dana had a large family — three sons and four girls. Unfortunately, three of them are already gone — lost at an early age from various causes. His daughters were the most beautiful girls that I have ever seen. His middle son, Peter, was also a wood-carver. In fact, he is a master wood-carver. I'll talk about him in a bit.

Uncle Dana was partly responsible for the many fights during my childhood. You see, my dad was a pacifist. He wouldn't hurt a fly — despite being a Marine in the Pacific during WWII. On the other hand, Uncle Dana believed that boys should stand up for themselves — learn to take their lumps. Dana had been in the Navy during WWII. He had no qualms about handling bullies. I was a small kid. I couldn't have weighed more than sixty lbs. during grade school — maybe less. Consequently, I got picked on a lot by the bigger boys. Uncle Dana was at the house at Willard Beach one day when I came home from the fourth grade. I had been picked on by a gang of kids who went to Henley School. Now, Dad wouldn't have done anything but tell me to "turn the other cheek." However, Dana was not Dad. He pulled me aside away from my mother and told me to stand my ground when faced with bullies. He taught me how to throw a punch. He showed me how to ball my fist and throw it straight from my shoulder. He showed me how to stand so as to keep my balance. That's all there was to it

— stand your ground — ball your fist — keep your balance — and throw straight from the shoulder. Oh, you also had to aim for their nose. A straight punch on the nose ended most fights. It hurt — it stunned — and the nose bled a lot, which scared the hell out of most kids. It wasn't long before I put his training to the test. I was stopped and harassed by three boys on the way home from Henley. They pushed and shoved and called me names. I swallowed hard, balled my fist, and hit Chester Monroe on the end of his nose. It stopped him cold. One of the other boys got a jolt on his nose as well. From then on, those boys no longer bothered me. However, that was the beginning of my new "problem."

Two things happened after that day. One — every other boy in the school went after me. I was like the gunfighter in the old west whose reputation drew gunslingers from far and wide — only on a grade school level. But, Uncle Dana's training stopped most of them in their tracks. The trick in a one punch fight was to be first — the first to throw a punch to the other kid's nose. That usually ended it. The second thing that happened was that I tried to solve every issue with my new-found tool. Got a problem with somebody? A bop on the nose was the response. I was a kid with a new, but very limited, tool. As they say, when you only have a hammer in your tool box, everything looks like a nail. I was bopping everybody on the nose — even my good friend, David Lovejoy (sorry, David). That went on for years — that is, until someone else did the same thing to me. There must have been more than one "uncle" out there showing kids how to throw a punch. After Vietnam, I became more of a pacifist like Dad. I'm pretty peaceful these days.

Dana's second son, Peter Q. Libbey, started carving wood when he was in grade school. After a stint in the Air Force, he opened a shop in the "Old Port" area of Portland in the seventies. That was before the renaissance of that area — there were still a lot of empty old brick buildings and run-down warehouses there then. Peter carved signs for a lot of the businesses that cropped up in the Old Port area before closing shop and working at home in the Maine woods. Peter is famous for his carved eagles. He is considered by many art critics to be "the finest carver of twentieth century American eagles" in the world. His carvings have been called "twentieth century masterpieces." His carvings are rarely for sale. When they are for sale, they command a very high price. Peter has also used his carving talents to sculpture the inside of wooden yachts, such as the 154 ft. sailing yacht, "Scheherazade." Wood carving must be in the "Libbey" family genes. Peter's son, William A. Libbey, carves contemporary eagles. He is also recognized as a "master."

CHAPTER 4

Aunt Dorothy

He was a British adventurer, an explorer and novelist whose travels took him around the world. He traveled to Mexico, Panama, and Central America. There, he claimed to have been wounded and captured by Pancho Villa, who forced him to become a spy. He swore he had discovered lost Indian tribes and "lost cities." He boasted of having found the "cradle of civilization" in Nicaragua and the lost civilization of "Atlantis." He displayed a "crystal skull" that he said he had uncovered in a cave in the deep jungles of Belize. In 1930, he held a weekly radio show on Sunday evenings in New York City, and spun his tales — entertaining and inspiring many thousands of listeners. His books became the basis for adventure movies; and many believed that he was the real "Indiana Jones." He was also my "great-uncle" — well, for a time. His name was Frederick Albert Mitchell – Hedges.

She was a "looker" — so deliciously attractive that men stopped whatever they were doing to gasp in her beauty. Her smooth, creamy skin, hazel eyes and shining brown hair complimented the delicate lines of her face and neck. She was athletic, healthy and vivacious, and could dance like Ginger Rogers — floating on the floor with the grace of an accomplished professional. As a teenager at Schenck High School in Millinocket, she had been voted the "Homecoming Queen." Boys tripped over themselves hoping to get a dance with her at the senior prom. She was intelligent and talented and had high aspirations — she wanted to go to the theater in New York. She dreamt of Hollywood and becoming an actress and movie star. She did — well, sort of. She was my "great-aunt" — Dorothy Aida Scott — my maternal-grandmother's sister.

In 1920, At the age of eighteen, Dorothy married Clyde Copp of Madison, Maine. Clyde was a few years older and an aspiring entertainer, who never made it out of Penobscott County. Before the marriage ended three years later, she gave birth to her only son, James. Her drive for fame and success was too powerful a drug to keep her in Maine. After her divorce, she left James in the care of her in–laws, borrowed a few dollars from her younger sister, Audrey, and struck out for New York City. I'm certain that men took advantage of her there. They made promises they couldn't possibly keep. They offered her money and — at times — shelter in return for her affection. For a time, she became a "chorus girl" — I think that was a polite way of putting it. She "danced" at the seedy Greenwich Village Club in Greenwich, New York City. It was there that she caught the eye of "Uncle" Frederick who was entertaining himself after returning from one of his many adventurous travels. Frederick was immediately smitten and begged the young divorcee to date him. She did. After a short time, they married. For their honeymoon they set off on an adventure trip to Cape Hatteras, where they planned to hunt and check out the indigenous species of birds and plants. They traveled to Mexico, South America, Panama, and Belize. They sought adventure together.

It took three years before "Aunt" Dorothy discovered that "Uncle" Frederick was already married to a woman in England. When she sued for divorce, she took the brunt of the publicity, with the newspapers calling her a "gold-digger." It didn't matter that F. A. Mitchell – Hedges was a bigamist; the papers went after her and not him. Distraught and disillusioned, she joined the Women's Army Corps where she served until after the end of World War II. Once the war was over, she followed her dream and moved to Hollywood where she was able to secure a position as a stand-in for actresses, such as Loretta Young. Like a lot of actresses, she had a number of short term, failed relationships, and marriages that ended in divorce.

When her career peaked, Aunt Dorothy became depressed. On the evening of the 26th of September 1959 — just as her friend, Marilyn Monroe, would — Dorothy swallowed a handful of barbiturates and ended her unhappy life. My Great-Aunt Dorothy Aida Scott's ashes were scattered somewhere on a beach in Southern California.

CHAPTER 5

Uncle Willy

Fisherman Lane flooded in the spring when the snow melted. A stream meandered downhill toward the beach from the fields behind Bathra's market on Willard Square. The stream paralleled Willow Street and formed a pond and marsh where the land flattened near the street's bottom. About a hundred yards from the beach, reeds and ca-tan-nine tails grew in the swampy marsh. The marsh became a bird paradise — with coots, mallards, and a few herons now and then. The air was full of insects and colorful dragonflies. There were thousands of black, squirming pollywogs under the lily pads. I loved to explore and catch frogs there. They were plentiful. I brought a few home or showed them to the girls in the neighborhood. They weren't impressed, though. I never had much luck with those girls. I don't know why.

From the pond, the stream trickled downhill and pooled in Bud Locke's yard and Fisherman Lane. The winding lane sits partially on the beach. Before the pumping station was built in the late seventies, there was no drainage. Water filled the lane from Willow to Willard street. In some places, it was waist deep — at least for us kids — maybe knee deep for adults. At times, we paddled boats in the muddy water in front of our house and the Locke's place. Uncle Willy lived in the second story across the lane from our house. He wasn't our uncle. He may have been someone's uncle, but he wasn't ours. He was just an old man who lived in the Locke's house. Their house was dilapidated with the front porch hanging to one side and wood planks on cement blocks for front steps. I can still see old Willy's balding gray-head hanging out the upstairs window. He made fun of us constantly. He listened to our conversations and mimicked everything we kids said. It was quite annoying. We had to play somewhere else to avoid his teasing. Uncle Willy only came out at night. When he did, we watched him pick through the trash barrels on the beach. He had a long stick with a nail on the end. He poked around in the barrels until he found something to eat. Once he found something, he limped back to the house and climbed the outside stairs that led to the second story. He did that for years and years. God only knows how he survived in the winter when there were no people on the beach to discard their garbage. I remember the day he died. The ambulance orderlies carried him down those outside rickety steps on a stretcher. It was quite a sight. We kids stood and stared with our mouths agape. I had never seen a lifeless body before. It's a good thing it was covered. I can only imagine what the inside of Willy's apartment looked like. The Locke's were hoarders. There must have been trash everywhere.

The Locke's house had many owners over the years. Some were quite eccentric. I remember one owner hung his deer kills from the branch of a big oak tree in their front yard. I guess he was showing his neighbors what a great hunter he was. Or, maybe it was just a convenient place. Another owner hung an auto engine block on a chain from the same tree branch. He left it there for six months or more. There were no regulations about those things back then. People left their old cars and appliances in their yards. Grass and weeds grew over them until they disappeared in the bushes. Abandoned lobster traps and buoys were buried in the grass and bushes behind a few houses. We never knew what we might find when we played hide-and-seek back there.

The Willard area was a slum in the fifties and sixties. Most folks were poor and still trying to recover from the war. All of the cottages were run down — left unpainted — their fences untended. Yards were full of weeds. Ours was better kept. But, it still had long yellow dandelions between mowing. Our front yard had a huge oak tree that I used to climb. All of the big oak and maple trees in the lane are gone now. Today, you would never know they were ever there. They were cut down many years ago because their branches hung too low. The lane was uneven, unpaved dirt and sand back then. In the summertime, cars got stuck in the sand as drivers attempted to cut through the lane. Drivers spun their wheels in futile attempts to get out, but they only dug their wheels in deeper. I helped a lot of drivers get unstuck from the sand. There were boards next to our house that I put under their back tires. With boards and a little rocking, I got them out.

Willard Beach is no longer a slum area. It's hard to believe that it's the same place. The marsh is gone. It's now a parking lot. The lane is paved and no longer floods. The old houses are still there, but most have had facelifts. Doctors and executives own many of the properties now. The Locke house looks brand new. I wonder if the owners know that Uncle Willy died there. I'd rather not know if I were them.

CHAPTER 6

Chick Wilder

The wind from the ocean blew the snow against the beach-side of our cottage. The cottage sat on a patch of ground we shared with another home owned by summer visitors — New Yorkers — they were "from away." We were surrounded there by sand on both sides of our adjoined-lots. The snow formed drifts against our tiny house and blocked our view of the bay from the cottage's porch windows. Ironically, the drifts provided an additional layer of insulation that helped shelter us from the cold wind. It was cold enough — nearly twenty below zero — so, we played on the icebergs that formed in Simonton Cove. That is, until David Lovejoy and I had to be rescued after we drifted out too far into the bay. The water was dangerously cold, and we would succumb to hypothermia in a matter of minutes if we fell. Our heavy winter coats, pant-suits, rubber-boots and woolen-mittens wouldn't have saved us. They would only weigh us down and pull us under the icy surface. The local fishermen weren't too happy about having to put a "punt" in the water from the "Point." They poled their way through that salty ice for several hundred yards to rescue us — two grade school kids — in trouble again.

David and Wesley Lovejoy, the Maxwell brothers and sisters — Robbie, Bruce, Jeffrey, Betsy and Mary — John Dube, I and many other kids slid down the packed snow and ice on Franklin Terrace — a steep one lane road that sloped from Preble Street down to Willard Beach. We maneuvered our sleds to the end of the street, where the hill petered out at the beach's entrance on Willow Street. At the bottom, we trudged back up the hill — repeating the process, again and again. We were all local kids — all baby boomers — all from families of modest means. Today, people would consider us "running wild." Yes, we were running free and unsupervised. That's the way things were back in the fifties. That's why growing up on the beach was so wonderful. Yes, it was wonderful — we lived at "Wonderful-Willard" — a true wonderland.

As we looked out our porch windows, the beach was framed perfectly — left, right, and center. History runs deep there. On the left — past the many cottages that dot the beach — are Fort Preble and the Spring Point Ledge Light. Fort Preble is an old fort — its construction began in 1808. It's what they call a "star fort" — built of stone, brick and sod. In its prime, its thick masonry walls contained fourteen heavy guns that pointed out to sea. Along with Fort Scammell on House Island — an island that from 1907 – 1937 was used as an immigration quarantine center like Ellis Island — it protected the entrance to Portland harbor during the War of 1812 and the Civil War. It was there at Fort Preble on the 15th of July, 1863, that Private Billy Laird earned the dubious honor of being the only Maine soldier to be executed for desertion during the Civil War. Although President Abraham Lincoln pardoned him, the telegraph message never made it to the fort. The wires were cut during the 1863 draft riots in Washington — very unfortunate for poor, homesick Billy, who faced that firing squad. The fort's grounds also contain the Thrasher Burying Grounds — the Old Settlers' Cemetery — South Portland's oldest landmark. Spring Point Ledge Light, the "sparkplug" lighthouse — constructed in 1897 — is connected to the fort by a 900-foot breakwater made from 50,000 short tons of granite. The lighthouse was intended to stop the ships from running aground on Spring Point Ledge. The lighthouse's fog-bell sounds every twelve seconds; at night, the sweeping beam of light from its lantern can be seen for miles.

In the center, just beyond the white, sandy beach is the ocean. Beginning a mile off shore, forested islands stretch out on both sides of — and behind — House Island. There are islands as far as the eye can see. They are part of what are sometimes referred to as the "Calendar Islands" — just short of 365 islands off Maine's rocky coast in Casco Bay. On the right of the beach is a jut of land we call the "Point." The Point is a finger of rocky high ground that protrudes out into the ocean. Simonton Cove was a working fishing-village back in the early days. The Point was where the lobstermen stowed their gear in fishing shacks. That's where they piled their lobster "pots." Its breakwater — a ragged line of black, jagged rocks, loosely and haphazardly piled together — points north toward Fort Preble and the lighthouse. The Point together with its breakwater, the islands, and Fort Preble — with the lighthouse and its breakwater — protect the semi-circular Simonton Cove from most of the heavy waves and weather. It was the perfect place for lobstermen to moor their boats. Today, out-of-staters pay a pricey fee to moor their pleasure boats there.

In the spring, once the snow drifts disappeared, once the icicles on the cottage's eaves melted, and the sand on the beach softened — the beach became a playground. We used to play tackle football bare-foot there. The sand was still damp and cold, but we were "Mainers" — anything above sixty degrees seemed warm to us. It was there on the beach, while playing football, where I "tackled" my first girlfriend — someone I have never forgotten. It was the best tackle of my life. With the snow and ice gone, the names painted on the rocky side of the Point revealed themselves. Local kids had hand-painted their graffiti there, with hearts and arrows and the names of their girlfriends below. It took years to wear that runny, multi-colored paint away. Of course, I wouldn't have a clue who painted those rocks — honest! The initials were just a coincidence.

To me, there was nothing better than summer at the beach. When I awoke, I could smell the ocean, hear the sea gulls, the rhythmic breaking of the waves against the shore, and the clang of the bell-buoys. If the fog hadn't yet lifted, I would hear the fog horn from Two-Lights, a set of lighthouses several miles away to the south. Back then, before the city stopped grooming the beach, the sand was pure white — today, it has largely been taken over by patches of dune grass that the environmentalists have deemed to be sensitive habitats. When the tide rolls out, it reveals the cove's slate-gray bottom. It becomes a huge, solid mudflat once the ocean recedes. The tide rolls back almost to the end of the breakwater. For me, when the tide went out, it was a great time to go "clamming."

All I had to do was find their tiny holes in the mud, jump up and land with my feet on both sides of the hole. When I landed, water would squirt into the air, letting me know that's where a clam was. Those razor clams are strong suckers —you have to dig fast and pull hard to get them released from the mud! If you like seafood, there are plenty of crabs and periwinkles on the breakwater rocks. Not everyone likes boiled periwinkles — it's an acquired taste — sort of like escargot.

When I was a kid, I really wanted to be a lobsterman. I would hang out at the Point and watch them dressed in their flannel shirts, jeans and hip boots, tending their fishing gear at the point. The Bolton brothers owned one of the fishing shacks, and they were there almost every day when they weren't pulling pots. Mom hated it when she saw me there. Their language was earthy and colorful — too colorful for a nurse. She had other plans for me. Women just didn't understand— these were lobstermen! As I told you, Simonton Cove was a working fishing village back then — back before they turned the Point into a park and began taxing everything — including the moorings and view of the ocean. Back then, lobstermen didn't have to pay a fee to moor their boats in the cove. They just dropped a cement block tied to some strong line into the water and marked their spot with a uniquely colored buoy. No one gave them any grief about it. When they wanted to scrape the barnacles off their boat's hull, they drove their trucks down the beach and dropped a boat cradle on the mud at low tide. When the tide rose back high enough, they drove their boats onto the cradles and hauled them up onto the beach. Once the barnacles were off, they would put a fresh coat of paint on the bottoms. No one ever thought about stopping them. It was normal, just as normal as us kids "running wild." They could leave their boats there on the beach as long as they wanted — many did. After all, they were the farmers of the sea. They were putting food on our tables.

Of course, during summer days, the beach became Portland's popular place to go swimming, sun-bathing, and boating. Dave Lovejoy, Peter Jensen, Phil Upton and I would sneak over to the far side of the Point where we would dive from the rocks. It was a beautiful place. We could see Portland Headlight — Maine's iconic lighthouse — from the Point. Now, we had to be careful that the lifeguard didn't catch us though! Grant "Chick" Wilder was the lifeguard during the summer. He ruled the beach, and we wanted to stay on his good side.

Chick was a striking figure with his deep, dark tan, jet-black hair, dark sunglasses, white lifeguard pith hat, and bathing trunks with the red cross. Chick was the official lifeguard and unofficial mentor for just about every kid in South Portland. He knew the names of all the kids on the beach and kept us under control. Kids — young and old — followed him around the beach and bath house like ducklings following their mother. When we heard his whistle blow, we knew it was time to get off the rocks and head back to safe territory. So, when I told you that we kids were "running free and unsupervised," well, I was stretching it a little. You see, Chick had "adopted" all of us kids — taken us under his wing. Today, adults wouldn't trust their children around older men. But, there was nothing to worry about with Chick. Generations of kids grew up under his supervision — hell, he was the lifeguard there for thirty-five years!

When we were old enough to start grade school, Chick taught us how to swim. He had all the kids line up on the beach just before the shoreline. He had us all swim in the sand in unison. He would pace back and forth that line of kids, correcting our strokes and showing us how to kick. Once he was satisfied that we had mastered the basic techniques and had developed our muscle memories, he would have us wade knee deep into the icy water and blow bubbles. Then he had us wade out until we were chest deep in the cold water and swim with our arms — blowing bubbles — while standing up. Finally, Chick would take us individually. He would support us with one hand under our chests while we put all limbs in motion, stroking and kicking. It didn't take long before we begged Chick to let us go on our own. That's how we learned to swim. Later, Chick held classes on the beach on the various swimming techniques — backstroke, breaststroke, scissor-kicks, and drown-proofing. He taught us water safety and boat safety and showed us the basics of first aid. The amazing thing was, Chick's primary job was working at night in the rail-yard. Life-guarding was his daytime hobby. When he wasn't working on the rails or at the beach, Chick led the kids' drum and bugle corps — the Dirigo Jets. So, many kids knew him from there and followed him to the beach.

At some point, Chick became something more to me than a mentor. He watched me grow up and took an interest in my development. When he thought that my mother had been a little too rough in disciplining me, he would stop by the house and let her know that maybe she should lighten up a bit. He could see the bruises on my back and arms. Mom was "old-school," and was only following what she had learned at the Good Will Home growing up — that sparing the rod, spoiled the child. Chick suggested other means of discipline. When Chick learned that I had picked the lock on the bath house, he pulled me aside and counseled me in private on the importance of being a good citizen. He never squealed or held it against me.

I could write a book about Chick and it wouldn't do him justice. One of my proudest moments was when I returned from Hawaii and told Chick that I had been selected to become a Presidential Pilot. That's when this picture of us together was taken in 1984. Chick was a beloved figure there on that beach and in South Portland. So beloved, that there's a monument dedicated to him at the end of Willow Street in front of the bath house — a monument put there by the kids who loved him.

Sometimes, I wonder who's there now watching out for the kids at Wonderful-Willard.

CHAPTER 7

A Working Life

Prior to attending my forty-fifth high school reunion, I made the mistake of mentioning something political on Facebook. It caused a row. While at the reunion, an old friend decided to raise the issue. She didn't think that I was sympathetic or understood the plight of poor people. She made the comment that I couldn't understand because I was privileged as a kid. I guess I was privileged. However, not in the way you may think. My parents grew up at the Good Will Home in Hinckley, Maine. They were both children of single mothers whose husbands died young as a result of alcoholism. They were fortunate to have been sent to the Hinckley home where they got a decent education. However, Good Will was a boarding school where they believed in hard work. They weren't given anything — they had to work for everything. They had to tend the farm's animals. Dad fed them and shoveled their manure. Mom helped with the cooking, laundry and cleaning. They had many other chores when they weren't in school. They weren't paid anything. They worked for their room and board. As a result, they didn't believe in giving their kids an allowance. But, they "allowed" us to work while we were growing up. I worked my entire life until I retired two years ago.

When Jerry Holt and I in were in the third grade at Willard Elementary School, the Fuller-Brush man picked us up after classes. We ran door to door delivering magazines for a penny a piece. We ran up and down flights of stairs in the many apartment buildings in Portland. We ran all over South Portland and Portland. By the end of each day, we made several dollars between us. During the winter, I shoveled driveways around the neighborhood for as little as 25 cents. In Maine, there were always plenty of places that needed to be shoveled. During the summers, I pushed my lawn mower up Willard Street looking for yards that needed mowing.

For 25 cents, I mowed people's lawns with a push lawn mower — the kind without a motor. I combed the beach and collected bottles. I returned them to Bathras' Market for two cents each. I worked for the Baptist church. They sent kids out to clean garages and attics. They also gave us other small jobs to do for the church members for a nominal fee.

In junior high school, I got a paper route. David Lovejoy and I split a route that used to be worked by the Doyle brothers. We picked our papers up at Flynn's candy store at the corner of Willow and Preble Streets. We trudged through waist deep snow in below zero temperatures during the winter. Our route covered the streets intersecting Willow Street and all of the streets surrounding Loveitt's field. Collecting money was the hardest part. The paper didn't bill customers back then. We went door to door in the evenings trying to get what was owed. We had to pay the paper company. We rarely broke even.

I got my first steady job while a freshman in high school. I washed dishes after school and in the evenings until closing at the Deering Ice Cream shop on Broadway. They paid me $1.00 per hour. It was tough work for a kid. I had to hustle when the place got busy. It really got busy after basketball games and football games — games that I rarely got to attend. I spent my summer days inside washing dishes and working at the takeout window when things really got busy. I didn't get to spend time at the beach.

I had several other jobs in the summer while in high school. My parents sent me to the "Word of Life Inn" on Schroon Lake in New York. There, I worked in the laundry, washing and folding sheets, pillow cases and towels. I also worked in the hotel's kitchen — scrubbing pots and washing dishes for ten dollars every two weeks. Although I didn't have a driver's license, I got a job parking cars in Portland at the Porteous Mitchell and Braun parking lot. I had to park the cars and collect the money as customers left. Richard Hale and I worked at cold storage in Portland on Commercial Street. We handled everything from fish to blueberries. It was freezing cold. We had to bundle up in heavy coats and boots while working in the refrigerated storage areas. Even bundled, we were still cold.

I worked there for several summers until I tipped a forklift over and crushed my foot. I wasn't supposed to be on the forklift; so, there was no compensation.

I volunteered for the draft in the fall of 1967 and left for Army basic training at Fort Dix, New Jersey in January of 1968. I spent two years in the Army with a tour in Vietnam from July 1968 – July 1969. I started at eighty dollars per month. I spent six months in Texas at Fort Hood. I completed my two-year military obligation in January of 1970. After the army, I found a job at Mercy Hospital as a surgical technician. After being trained by nuns and nurses, I made $1.75 an hour. I worked during the day and went to the University of Maine at night. It was there that I met my wife. Barbara was a student nurse at Mercy. I quit Mercy after about two years and worked at the Boy's Training Center in South Portland for about six months as a counselor. The counselor position was basically a babysitting position for troubled teenage boys. I made two dollars an hour there. I left for Memphis State University in January of 1972. I lived in the dormitory and worked in a factory at night doing piece work. I cut felt automobile trunk-liners after they came off a press for three dollars per hour. While other kids went home or to Fort Lauderdale for Spring break, I hid in the dorm. I couldn't use the lights for fear of getting caught. I had to sneak in and out to get food.

I completed one semester at Memphis State before getting married. Barbara, and I moved to Memphis in August. I painted houses while working my way through college. I made one hundred dollars a week. It was difficult work. We worked on ladders scraping and painting. When my landlord saw me painting my apartment, he hired me to paint all of the duplexes on our street. I charged one hundred dollars to paint the inside of his one and two-bedroom apartments. Combined with the GI Bill and Barbara's nursing job, we made enough to completely pay for my tuition. After graduation from college, I inventoried merchandise at a retail store in Memphis. Fed up with working in retail, I joined the Marine Corps in March of 1975. I stayed for nearly twenty years as a helicopter pilot. I spent two years at sea flying off of aircraft carriers in the Mediterranean and the Pacific. I flew for the White House and worked my way up to Squadron Commander. I retired as a Lieutenant Colonel in 1994.

After the Marine Corps, I worked briefly at Radio Shack as an assistant manager while looking for decent work. After a few weeks of low pay, I took a temporary position as a superintendent at Matson Terminals where I supervised the loading and unloading of ships for twenty dollars per hour. There, I worked my way up to Vessel Operations Manager. After five years at Matson, I transferred to another terminal operated by Stevedoring Services of America. I worked various superintendent positions in Vessel Operations and in the terminal's Yard for seven years. In 2006, I went back to work for the Marine Corps with Science Applications International Corporation as a military analyst. I worked as an analyst for nine and a half years in Yuma, Arizona. I retired three years ago at the age of sixty-six.

Yes, I guess I was privileged. I've never been unemployed until now. I don't talk politics anymore. There's no point. We all have our own realities.

CHAPTER 8

My Band

He gingerly guided that old, black, '57 VW Bug with the oval rear window through the dirty slosh of ice and snow. We passed the Congregational Church and Mount Pleasant Cemetery at the top of "Meeting House Hill." He had me trapped! Dad was taking advantage of this rare opportunity to give me another lecture on the importance of school work. Oh, how I hated school back then. I didn't have that burning desire to become a doctor like my older brother, "Pete." I spent most of my time in school day-dreaming. Or, in high school, I stared at the pretty girls in their gym shorts, playing tennis on the courts outside the school's windows. Man, what a sight! It was another seven years before I finally got interested in school. It was almost too late. We made the left turn at the corner light — passing "DiPietro's market." By the way, DiPietro's market makes great "Italians." if you're ever in the "Willard" area of South Portland, get one of those unique sub-sandwiches at DiPietro's. You can't get those "Italians" anywhere else. You won't find the bread, those sour pickles, or that special dressing anywhere outside of Maine. Now, back to our story.

Dad and I headed down Pillsbury Street past "Willard School" on our right. The school is not there anymore. It was torn down around 1972. The land is now a park. The city named it after Mr. Sam DiPietro, the owner of the market. I attended kindergarten and grades one through three at Willard. That's where my dislike for academics began. An "A" on a report card meant something different then. An "A" at Willard meant, "Parents, Should Make an Appointment to see the Teacher." My parents knew all my teachers by their first names before I left Willard. I will say one thing about the education system back then, though. The teachers in South Portland were tough! They didn't coddle us. God forbid that we should get sent to the Vice Principal's Office. There were no rules against corporal-punishment back then — at least none that were enforced. I really got paddled in the Mahoney Junior High office. Plus, when my parents got wind of my behavior, I got paddled again when I got home. The teachers were strict. They made us write cursive. We had to take French, Spanish and Latin. Hell, most of today's kids can't write their own names or speak English. In high school, we had "minimum requirements" — a list of words and things that you had to know or spell correctly before you were allowed to don that graduation cap and gown. I'm not bragging, 'cause God only knows that I wasn't an "A" student — except maybe at Willard School and college. But, let's slow down; I'm getting ahead of myself.

As we rode down the hill headed toward "Wonderful-Willard" beach, something on the radio caught my attention. I turned up the volume on the bug's AM radio. As I did, I heard two disc jockeys on WJAB — Portland's "Top forty" radio station. They were discussing an upcoming show at Portland's Frye Hall on Saturday. I didn't mean to be impolite or interrupt Dad, but they were "hyping" my band — the "Mad Hatters!" I can't imagine what was going through Dad's mind as he sat next to me trying to get through my thick skull while I fixated on the radio. If I had known more about his life, I might have paid more attention. But, I was sixteen years old and stupid. Besides, they were talking about my band. I had become famous! At least that's what I thought in that thick skull full of mush.

Sometime in the fall of 1965, I was bored with school and bought a bass guitar. I saw it hanging in the window of a music store in Portland on Congress Street. I fell in love. It wasn't a Fender or a Gibson, it was a Kent. It didn't matter. I had no idea how to play it, anyway. I was in the South Portland High School and Mahoney Junior High School Bands. I played trombone — well, more like played at playing. I hated to practice. There were too many distractions. I was sixteen years old and lived on a beach. Who the hell wanted to stay inside? No one I knew; except maybe my brother, Pete. He loved playing the trumpet. He was so good at it, you could hear him playing all the way to the "Point." Pete was good at everything he did. But for me, playing a trombone wasn't cool. I wanted to be in a band like the Beatles. I got my opportunity when one of the local high school rock bands broke up. All bands eventually break up — except maybe the Rolling Stones. There's always conflict and jealousy. Every band has a story that's very similar. Anyway, when the band broke up, some wanted to go their own way with new members. I joined a band that needed a bass player. It didn't matter that I didn't know how to play. The bass was the easiest of the guitars to learn. It has four strings and is symmetrical — meaning that the same patterns apply anywhere on the neck of the guitar. Once you learn the patterns, you can play just about any song. Neil Stilphen was the lead guitar player and taught me the basics. Neil was good. Neil's older brother, Wayne, played rhythm guitar. David Dodge played the drums. David was probably the only real musician in the group. He may have been the best percussionist in Maine at the time. He was that good. We could have played "Wipe Out" as our only song, and the fans would love it. David played it as good as the Surfaris' drummer did on their original hit. We went through a few lead singers in the Mad Hatters. Our first, after Steve Luttrell departed, was Bob Brown — a senior in the class of '65. Bob really got into it. He could belt out a song — and he really impressed the disc jockeys. They went on and on about how good Bob was while hyping the band on the radio. Peter Jensen fronted the group after Bob left. But, by then we were close to breaking up. That's what bands do. Stan McLaughlin replaced Wayne Stilphen on the rhythm guitar. Stan was a good-looking kid who attracted a lot of girls. Unfortunately, he was also a sensitive kid. After high school, Stan got involved in drugs. He quickly went from experimentation to becoming a hard-core user of the more dangerous drugs available in Portland. Stan committed suicide in 1977. He was distraught over a girl. He put a shotgun to his chest on her steps in Portland and pulled the trigger. Such a waste.

We played a lot of venues in '65. We played at Portland City Hall. We played at a lot of high school graduations and private parties. We opened for a lot of big groups — such as the McCoys at City Hall. Remember "Hang on Sloopy?" That was the McCoys. We got to go back stage after we finished and chat with them and other bands. The performance I remember the most — the one that sticks in my mind — was at Frye Hall in Portland. I was interested in a girl from high school back then. But as usual, she didn't want anything to do with me. You'll hear that a lot in my stories. I was pretty skinny and not very attractive. Girls weren't interested in my unique looks. She turned me down several times when I asked for a date. Well, our band played at Frye Hall after a lot of hype from the WJAB disc jockeys. A lot of young kids — mostly girls — showed up to watch and dance. Our band was a hit. The girls went wild. They cheered us on and asked for more. While I was on stage, I saw the girl I asked out watching us with her date. She stood mesmerized — staring at the band. When we were finished playing our first set, we went back stage and took a side door out to the audience. It was sweet! Young girls surrounded me and asked for my autograph. As I signed my name on their scraps of paper, I saw her. She was standing alone. Her date was gone. I gave her a nod and continued signing. Then, I went back stage and got ready for the next set. Life was sweet.

CHAPTER 9

My First Girlfriend

I pulled my wool ski cap over my ear so the phone's cold earpiece wouldn't sting so much. A few nickels, and I was walking on air — floating among the clouds. Heaven was on the other end of the line.

I trudged a half mile through the snow in twenty below zero weather to call her. There was no privacy at home. We had a party line. The old, black Bell telephone was connected to the wall in our living room. If someone heard my awkward attempts at wooing her, they might make fun. It was much easier humiliating myself in the freezing cold. I had to break the ice and snow away from the phone booth's door; but that was ok. I would have made the walk barefoot.

The girl I called wasn't real. She was there, but I couldn't hear her. I heard an illusion. I never really knew her inner being. I heard what I wanted to hear — something totally different. I hadn't fallen in love with her. I had fallen in love with an idea that just happened to include her. It could just as easily have been someone else. I let it be her, because I wanted to fall in love, and she was on the other end of the line. At sixteen, love is truly blind.

When we met, it was fall. We were on the beach with other high school kids. She was fifteen. There was a chill in the air. We played football barefoot in the cold, damp sand. One tackle, and I was gone. I was blinded by what I thought I saw. I wouldn't see reality again for years. I couldn't get her out of my mind — not her, the illusion. I still see her in my dreams.

What she wanted was not what I thought she wanted. She never really wanted my advances. I only wanted her to want them. She didn't want to be treated like a princess. She wanted something totally different. What it was I never really knew or understood. I think she was more adventurous, more spirited than me. We were both too young.

We dated as young kids do. We went to movies. We went to the beach. We went skiing where I made a fool of myself. We stayed home and watched television. We had a standing Friday night date. She even rode to Fort Dix with my parents while I was in Army boot camp. We wrote letters. But, there were others who saw her — others who saw the same beauty that I saw. I wasn't there to hold on. There were too many suitors. She was much too young to wait.

As you might have suspected, it didn't last long — a year or two at most. It ended as young love always does. You can't hold on to an illusion.

When I went to war, it was over. She met another. I was devastated. She wrote. She still wanted to be friends. But, to me it was all or nothing. I returned her letters. I was such a fool. It took years to put things in perspective. As I slept in the far-off jungles of Vietnam, I held her tightly in my arms and kept our love alive in my dreams.

CHAPTER 10

A Ski Trip

I scraped the frost off the inside of the VW bug's windshield. We stopped several times to scrape the ice off the outside windows. We drove and slid on the snow-laden Maine roads. There was no heat in that VW — not even enough to defrost the windows. Our hands and feet were frozen. She sat next to me — her parka's hood over her blond head. Most girls bailed when they saw the car I was driving — not her. She was a trooper. Maine girls are like that. Well, not all of them. I was lucky. She was used to the cold. But, at below zero temperatures, love can only go so far. Who could blame her for wanting a warm ride? Yet, she was still with me.

We were headed to Rangeley. She was a skier. I wasn't. I couldn't afford to own the skis or the boots. They were expensive for a high school kid back in the sixties. With my dishwashing job, I could barely afford the lift tickets and gas to get us there. We were frozen when we pulled into the lodge's parking lot. She went right for the slopes. I didn't blame her. She needed to warm up after that ride. I rented some skis and went for the bunny run while she was on the intermediate slope. I prayed she wouldn't see me as I started down the hill. Little kids and toddlers waved as I passed. I was in trouble. No one taught me how to snow plow. As I picked up speed, I panicked. I went too fast and didn't know how to slow down or stop. So, I sat down. I dragged my butt between my skis and tried to dig my poles in the snow. It didn't help. I kept going. It didn't take long to reach the bottom. Before I did, I nearly hit some kids who walked toward the lodge. At the end of the slope, I slammed right into the side of the building. I nearly broke my neck. People laughed and pointed. That was enough for me. For the rest of the day, I stuck around the lodge at the bottom of the bunny trail. I tried to look cool and nonchalant. I tried not to fall down.

At the end of the afternoon, we rejoined. "How was it for you, David?" she asked. "Oh, it was great! Sorry I missed you; I guess I got carried away having so much fun on the expert trail," I said. That was the end of my skiing days.

We scraped the bug's windshield on the way back to South Portland. I dropped her off at Kelsey Street. What a date!

CHAPTER 11

Uncle Malcolm

In the winter of 1968, having volunteered for the draft, I was in Army basic training at Fort Dix, New Jersey. I was eighteen years old. Near the end of boot camp, I caught pneumonia, probably from doing pushups in the snow with my shirt off. Back then, exercising partially clothed in the cold was quite common during boot camp. I spent at least a week in the Army hospital at Fort Dix recovering.

Shortly after leaving the hospital and returning to the company, my head Drill Instructor, a big scary looking man, escorted me to the company office. Getting called to the company office during basic training is never a good thing for a Private. It usually means that you have screwed up and will spend hours standing at attention waiting to be yelled at by the company First Sergeant or face charges of some kind. There was also a likely possibility that I could be recycled — meaning transferred and having to start training from the beginning with a new group of recruits. It was looking grim, and I was not a happy camper.

When I entered the company office, I was met by a group of immaculately dressed Drill Instructors. They looked mean, but they were not yelling. In fact, they showed no emotion at all. They had my dress uniform and shoes in hand. At the same time, the company commander — a Captain — was poring over my skimpy service record. While I stood at attention, they discussed among themselves my performance on the rifle range, my physical fitness results, and whether I had completed enough training to graduate with my class. I thought I was screwed. After twenty minutes or so of being scrutinized by this serious looking group of DI's, one of them took me to the barber shop and waited while I got a free, fresh buzz-haircut. When I was finished, he took me back to the barracks and waited while I showered and shaved. After shaving, we went back to the company office. Once again, I was greeted by the intimidating group of DI's. I was told to put my dress uniform on, and the DI's pored over me, making sure that I was properly dressed and my uniform fit perfectly. They even checked my ears and fingernails. I had no idea what was going on, but there wasn't anything I could do but stand at attention while they adjusted my tie and touched up the shine on my shoes. When they were finished and satisfied that I was presentable in my dress uniform, the company commander and several DI's drove me to the Fort Dix Headquarters. I still had no idea what was happening, but now my imagination was running wild with the possibilities — re-cycle, court-martial, separation? The anticipation had me in a cold sweat.

After arriving at the Fort Dix Headquarters with a DI on each side of me, I was escorted to the Commanding General's office. Now, I knew I was in deep trouble. This was like being escorted to a firing squad! As we climbed the stairs to the General's office, I tried to think what I had done that could possibly have warranted so much attention. I couldn't remember anything other than a few discrepancies during the last inspection. But, then again, it didn't seem to take much to upset these frowning people with the Smokey Bear hats.

Reaching the top of the stairs, things changed. I was introduced to a woman with three children. Two were baby girls. One was barely a year old, and the other couldn't have been more than two. There was also a little boy dressed in an Army uniform. I had just met my Aunt Carol Libbey and my cousins, her three children—Tommy, Maryann, and Christine. After a few minutes, we were escorted into the Commanding General's office where my Aunt was presented with a Purple Heart for her husband, Malcolm P. Libbey, who had been killed in Vietnam in October of 1967. As we stood there in the office, I held one of Carol's squirming baby girls, Maryann, in my arms, while Carol accepted the Purple Heart from the Commanding General.

After graduation from boot camp and further training at Fort Benning, Georgia, I was shipped off to Vietnam. I never saw Aunt

Carol or her three children again. That is until more than thirty-five years later, I read a story about a woman who was associated with children of KIA's who had never known their fathers. It was Maryann, the restless baby I had held in my arms in the General's office so many years before. Somehow, after lot of searching, I managed to get in contact with her. She was a widow with two boys living in Philadelphia.

Years later, after brief correspondence, Maryann invited me to participate in the reading of the names at the Vietnam memorial. I had only been there once, and it had been an emotional experience — one that I didn't care to repeat. The names of a few friends from high school and many from the Army were inscribed on that wall. There's something about seeing their names that brings out repressed feelings and makes their loss seem so much more real. I agreed to meet her there anyway.

When the day came to meet Maryann at the wall, I realized that we had not agreed where to meet, and I had no idea what she looked like. I had only seen a grainy photo of her in the paper taken during one of her appearances with the children of KIA's. Arriving at the wall, my intuition took over, and I looked up Uncle Malcolm's information in the directory that stood near the wall. Malcolm Pierce Libbey, Rockland, Maine was there. His name is located on panel 27E, line 96, next to the soldier who died with him October 12, 1967, PFC Jose Salazar from Lansing, Michigan. I started walking in that direction. Arriving at the spot, there was a crowd of people nearby, but off to the side stood a beautiful, tall lady. She was elegantly dressed, standing alone and holding a red rose with her back to me facing the wall. I called her name. She turned and smiled, then started crying. Once again, more than thirty-five years later, I held Maryann in my arms. We held the rose under her father's name and had someone take our picture. Later, we climbed up the stairs to the stage, and I stood with her as she read the names on her list to the audience below. It was an emotional experience for her, and it took all I had to hold back the tears in my eyes when she broke down reading her father's name, "Malcolm Pierce Libbey."

Maryann's father, my father's brother—my uncle — Staff Sergeant Malcolm Pierce Libbey, was a hero. He was awarded the Silver Star posthumously for heroism in Vietnam. The DI's who groomed me that day in boot camp knew it. They had served with him. He had also been a DI, one of them. The Army named a building after him — Building 6573, Libbey Hall, at Fort Knox, Kentucky. But to me, the real heroes were his late wife, Carol, and his children — Malcolm Jr, Donna, and Richard from his first marriage, and Tommy, Christine, and of course, Maryann. Like so many others, they grew up and survived this harsh world without the help of a father.

CHAPTER 12

Mortars

It came unexpectedly. It was a black night. We were at an encampment near a village surrounded by rice paddies, banana trees and heavy vegetation. I ventured out of the bunker to relieve myself. I was alone. It caught me off-guard, unprotected in the open. The sound of automatic assault rifles broke the silence. The unseen enemy fired from outside the perimeter at a Chinook helicopter that was attempting to land not more than a hundred yards away. There were streams of green tracers shooting up against the black sky. The helicopter waved off and departed. Almost immediately, the rifle sounds were followed by mortar rounds. I could hear them as they left the tubes — they made a tooping sound. "Toop, Toop." Seconds later the rounds exploded. They were landing all around me. I couldn't move. I couldn't get my legs to work. I was frozen. As I hugged the ground, the buttons on my shirt felt like mountains. With each explosion, I twitched and nearly rose off the ground. It went on for what seemed like eternity. Mortar rounds tooping and exploding. There was nothing I could do. There was no one to shoot. There was no one to help. It was my first time under fire. I was 19 years old. I was scared to death.

There were many more days and nights like that. I guess I can't forget. It's the strangest things that bother me. The ring of a telephone — a backfire — firecrackers — things moving in my peripheral vision. These things cause me to jerk involuntarily. They cause my heart rate to increase. They make me angry. When they do, I have to tell myself that it's ok. It's only that stupid war. Take a deep breath. Try to relax. Don't over react. Don't scare your wife.

She's aware. She knows. She watches. She'll remind me. She prefers to drive. She gets uncomfortable when I jerk the wheel.

I tell her I don't like driving in California. The drivers are too impatient. They are all in a hurry. They get angry when you don't speed. They pass you on both sides. They weave in and out of traffic. I don't like it when she drives. She tail gates. She gets too close for the speed we are traveling. I squeeze the overhead handle. I tighten my seatbelt.

Just take me home.

CHAPTER 13

Cam Ranh Bay Hospital

I hovered above myself — floating in the air — looking down on the circle of soldiers kneeling around me. Simultaneously, I looked up from the mud — I looked in George Steven's eyes. A trickle of blood ran down George's forehead from a tiny piece of shrapnel. I watched a drip of his blood fall to my chest. I could see tears forming at the corners of his eyes. I could feel his emotional pain and sorrow. I felt as if I could read his mind — as if I could read all of their minds as they stared down at me.

It was the afternoon of the 19th of April, 1969 at Firebase Blaze — a 101st Airborne Division staging area in defoliated mountains east of the A Shau Valley in Vietnam. Eight of us were hit by the same blast. After the explosion, I staggered and fell to the ground. Unwounded soldiers tried to comfort me while talking among themselves. They thought I couldn't hear them — but I heard every word — every sound. They didn't think that I was going to make it — there were too many wounds. They whispered to themselves as if I couldn't understand what they were saying or thinking. They didn't know that I'd never had such mental clarity or felt such peacefulness in my life. I was ready to slip away. I felt myself falling deeper and deeper into a peaceful sleep. I felt as though my spirit was ready to rise up and leave my body. I was ready to leave the earth and Vietnam, but my friends wouldn't let me go. They yelled and slapped at my face. They wouldn't let me close my eyes. They wouldn't let me die. They kept me alive — and I was so ready to go — I was so tired — it would be such a relief — the pain was almost over — all my cares were nearly gone. All I had to do was close my eyes and let my spirit rise up.

Three weeks later, I was lying in my hospital bed. My back had been torn open by shrapnel, and my right arm had been pierced with hot metal fragments at the inside of my right elbow.

I was recovering from wounds at the 6th Convalescence Center at Cam Ranh Bay — my third and final hospital in lovely Vietnam. I was supposed to be convalescing. Initially, I spent several weeks in Army field evacuation hospitals. There, surgeons removed the shrapnel from my body and monitored my condition before sending me off to less intensive care facilities. I had been loaded onto jeeps, driven on dusty bumpy roads, and flown with patients stacked like cordwood in medevac planes. I was carted over half of the country before finally coming to rest there in that hospital by the sea. Pieces of shrapnel were still lodged in my chest and back. "They are too close to your heart and spine to remove," the surgeons said. The wounds on my back were left open to prevent infection. Once closed and healed, they would leave large keloid scars to remind me of my exploits.

Cam Ranh Bay was a multi-use Logistics Base. The Army used it to unload huge ships loaded with supplies. They also used it for military members to enjoy R&R — rest and recreation — time off from the fighting. It was a home for their convalescence hospital. So, at the same time that the big ships were off-loading, there were soldiers, sailors and Marines on R&R, rollicking in their bathing suits in the surf. At night the Army sponsored "boxing smokers," where enlisted men would pound each other silly in the ring. There were also several clubs that were open for all enlisted ranks. At the clubs you could enjoy the air-conditioning, escape the oppressive heat, and have a cold one with other teenagers. There were outdoor movies and Filipino Rock Bands that provided entertainment. Young, dark-haired girls danced in skimpy bikinis, sending frustrated males back to their tents with something to think about other than the war. Those patients whose wounds weren't serious enough for them to be sent to Japan or home, underwent convalescence therapy.

Now, the Army's idea of convalescence therapy was not the same as civilian convalescence! There were no pretty nurses supporting us as we struggled to regain mobility. No, the Army's way was to send the wounded out on sand-bag filling, or shit-burning details. Usually, a Sergeant — rifle in-hand would sit and watch us "patients" fill sand bags and stack them neatly around the hospital shacks. It was almost like being on a chain gang without the chains. Their favorite therapy was to have us drag fifty-gallon barrels — cut in half — out from under the two-hole out-houses that were scattered around the base. Once clear of these wooden structures, we would pour kerosene oil on the sweet stuff and light it on fire. Thick, black smoke would curl up in the air, and the stench would permeate our blue pajamas.

So, after a few weeks of convalescing at Cam Ranh Bay, I was ready to go back to my unit. There's only so much recuperation that one can tolerate. Besides, I hadn't had any mail or contact with my friends since the day they had loaded me on a stretcher and put me into a Huey helicopter at that fire support base overlooking the A Shau Valley. I was a lonely, 19-year-old teenager, and I wanted to either go home or get back to my unit. I wanted to be with my friends and get some mail.

I'll never forget the day that I rolled out of that hospital bed on my own. The bed was lying flat on a rectangle of sandbags in case we needed somewhere to hide from incoming mortar rounds. I put my blue pajama top on and strolled out of the shack, heading to the club. As I walked to the club, I could hear the roar of soldiers in the distance. They were cheering their favorite fighters in the boxing ring by the sea. Music blared from the beach. I reached the club and opened the wooden door. A rush of cool air hit me in the face. I saw an empty barstool with soldiers dressed in Army uniforms sitting on either side of it and went for it. After sitting at the bar and ordering a cold Budweiser beer, I stared at the bottles of beer on the shelves behind the bar. There, I unfocused my eyes, went into that 1000-yard stare, and dreamt of home.

Sitting there at the bar, dreaming of home, I thought I heard a familiar voice. The accent was that familiar Maine accent! You can recognize a Maine accent immediately. Words like, "wicked, cunning, and ayuh," are unique to Mainers. I turned to my right, and there were two soldiers laughing and talking on the stools next to me. I tapped the one next to me on the shoulder. As he turned and spun around on the stool, I recognized him instantly! It was

Tony Salamone from my hometown in South Portland, Maine! We had gone in the Army about a week apart and had both trained at Fort Dix at the same time beginning in January of 1968. Tony and I slapped each other's backs (ouch!), had some cold brews, and caught up on our adventures. Tony was heading off to Thailand for his three days of R&R.

I recently saw Tony at our fiftieth High School Reunion in South Portland, Maine. We caught up and reminisced about that day in the Cam Ranh Bay club forty-eight years ago. The odds of us meeting there were astronomical! But then again, I always seemed to beat the odds.

CHAPTER 14

Welcome Home

I took a taxi from the Army base to the airport. I was conscious of their dirty looks. No one bothered me. They just stopped and stared. I didn't give a shit. What could they do? Send me back to hell? This was nothing. I was numb anyway; I couldn't feel anything if I tried. I'd heard the stories.

When I arrived at the airport terminal, soldiers said, "You better take the uniform off!" I wouldn't. I couldn't. I didn't have any other clothes. Besides, my friends were still fighting and dying on Hill 996 as I waited to board the plane. The way I looked at it, these protestors weren't disrespecting me. They were disrespecting themselves. I wasn't ashamed of my uniform or the terrible things I had seen. I wore it with pride. I had a clear conscience. I thought, "These people have no clue. They have no idea. If they only knew."

I boarded the plane in San Francisco. The stewardess was polite and welcomed me onboard. I walked to my seat with my hat in hand. People leaned away in their seats. No one wanted to sit next to me on the plane. I guess they thought Vietnam was a contagious disease. That was ok. It gave me room to stretch out. I could sleep on my way home. I just kept to myself.

From New York to Portland the plane was smaller. I actually recognized someone. He was one of the corporate big wigs from my dishwashing days at the Deering Ice Cream shop. He welcomed me back home. I shook his hand. People watched. No one else said a word, they just stared. I thought, "So, that's how it's gonna be. That's ok. I've been through worse. I'll get through this too."

When I arrived at the Portland jetport, I took a taxi through Portland. I told the driver to pull over, I wanted to walk. I walked through the streets of Portland carrying my duffel bag. I couldn't believe how much it had changed in just one year. Some streets were one way. Others were rerouted. My Army uniform was a magnet. Young punks saw it and wanted to fight me. A gang of teens followed me through the town waiting for me to make a wrong turn. They had no idea. I was a watch that was wound too tight. I could snap at any minute. I got to the bottom of Congress Street before they jumped. Fists were flying from every direction. I blocked them as best I could. Some got through. Some of mine got through also. When it was over, I wiped my bloody nose, buttoned my torn shirt, and hailed a cab. It was 12th of July, 1969 — the same day my Army unit was recovering the bodies of twenty of our friends killed in action on Hill 996.

Welcome Home!

CHAPTER 15

Memory Boxes

My wife, Barbara, keeps "memory boxes." There are four tucked away in our home office closet in Trabuco Canyon, California. There's one for each of us — Barbara, me and our two daughters, Alicia and Merisa. They are kind of like scrap-books, containing things from important events in our lives — things that Barbara has saved over the past forty-five years of our marriage. My box has things like letters from my close friends, birthday cards, newspaper clippings, report cards, diplomas, napkins from special dinners, and obituaries of loved ones. Every once and a while, I dig into my box and pull out a memory. Some memories are special. Some, I would rather forget, but I keep anyway — I'm not sure why. They all have some unique meaning or some special feeling attached.

I've pulled this photo from my box a few times. It's one of the few things that I personally put there. It goes back almost fifty years. Barbara was always curious about why I insisted on keeping it. It's a portrait of a girl I barely knew from South Portland High School. It was her graduation photo taken during her Senior year in 1969. We never dated; and to be honest, I don't recall speaking with her all that much. Still, it will always have a special place in my box.

You see, although she was just a friend of an old girlfriend, fifty years ago, she threw me a life-line while I was in Vietnam. When other friends had stopped writing — I guess as a result of the events swirling around the country back then — she didn't stop. Letters from home were important, as I bet they are today to our soldiers, sailors, and Marines — those who are in harm's way. She even sent me this graduation photo.

So, before I put this photo back in my special place, I want to take a moment and thank a girl who I barely knew. She is an Angel from above. Thank you, Geri Post. I'll never forget your kindness. Dave

CHAPTER 16

Currahee Reunion

When I looked at the photograph, I saw it immediately. He was standing slightly to the right of us. There was just enough separation for me to notice. He was wearing a different T-shirt and had assumed the "broken-zipper-position," holding-hands-with himself. It made "Len" Griffin look alone and vulnerable. I guess in his mind he was alone. At least, that's what he thought forty-eight years ago while lying in the dirt with a bullet in his left shoulder and half of his left ear torn off. He was lying there with jungle insects crawling over his bloody face, waiting for the rescuers who didn't come. Twenty dead or dying soldiers, who he had never met before, were with him. Those still alive lay moaning, drawing their last, agonizing breaths. Bad luck had brought him to this spot. He had to replace a Forward Observer who had injured his leg jumping from a helicopter during the initial assault. Ten thousand miles from home, Len thought that we had all abandoned him. He would only live through the ambush by pretending to be dead. I imagine that sometimes he wished he hadn't made it. It would be forty gut-wrenching years of feeling betrayed by fellow soldiers before he learned the truth — brave men had tried to get back to him.

We got the call a few weeks earlier. Our former Platoon Leader, who we now affectionately call "Hap," invited us to be there. Of course, we didn't call him "Hap" back there in Vietnam! If we had, we might have ended up in the Long Binh stockade. You see, Hap had been a regular Army officer — an airborne ranger with paratrooper jump wings on his chest. There was a strict protocol in the Army in those days. It may have lightened up a little today; but back then, officers and enlisted folk didn't mix socially. So, when Hap put forth the "invitation," to us it was more like an order — well, sort of. We were all civilians now, but we would have done anything if Hap had asked us. That's the kind of respect we had for him. Hap had been different from the rest of our Leaders. When I say "different," I mean he didn't mind sharing a tent, or a foxhole, or a meal of C-rations with his men. Before Hap arrived, I never broke bread with an officer. It was strange when Hap moved right in to our tent in the middle of nowhere. I guess he felt like he had to keep an eye on his people. Great leaders are like that.

Hap had invited us to climb "Currahee Mountain," the three-mile-up and three-mile-back hill in Toccoa, Georgia, where our former outfit, the 1/506th of the 101st Airborne Division, trained before World War II. You may have seen it portrayed in the movie, Band of Brothers. It had a steep, winding path that paratroopers ran up and then back down in order to stay in shape. Hap and his friend, Lieutenant Colonel (Retired) Jim Tarleton, intended to honor their men — twenty soldiers who had died on Hill 996 on the 11th of July, 1969 — by having members of their unit make the climb. Hence, Hap put out the word for us to be there. It was Len's idea; but for us, it was Hap who made it happen.

Now, fortunately or not, not all of us were on that hill back then. A few had been on R&R — 3 days of rest and relaxation — a break offered after being in country for 6 months — or they were sent home. I was on the freedom plane at the time. This was the flight we all dreamed of that came at the end of our three hundred and sixty-five day tour. Unknowingly, I was heading home to a country in great turmoil and unrest. It would be forty years before I learned about what happened to my friends the day I left Vietnam. After Hamburger Hill — a ferocious fight on Dong AP Bia Mountain in the A Shau Valley — the Army didn't want any more bad publicity. Senator Ted Kennedy had seen to that by creating a firestorm in Congress and the media over the "waste" of American lives. So, the events on Hill 996 were kept quiet. When I got home to South Portland, Maine, I kept my head down. I remained silent, so as to be inconspicuous. Being a Vietnam veteran was not in vogue back then. I was too overcome by events to think of contacting my buddies; I didn't have the heart to tell them what to expect when they got home — that they were despised by their fellow Americans.

We arrived in Cumming, Georgia on the day before the climb. Hap insisted that we stay at his beautiful home in an upscale gated area by a lake. As we arrived, we were greeted by Hap's beautiful bride, Barbara, and their little dogs and cat. We were much older, gray-headed or balding, chests just above the belt-lines. But, when I looked at my fellow soldiers, I saw them as the teenagers they were forty-eight years ago. Barbara put on a beautiful spread of food, and Hap had an endless supply of any beverage that we wanted. Hap kept busy washing the dishes, with Barbara waiting on us as though we were all celebrities. We spent the afternoon and evening doing things that old soldiers do — reminiscing, hugging, and saying how much we loved one another. I apologized for losing touch. They all understood. We all had faced the same thing coming home. It was no big deal. I felt the weight lifted from my shoulders.

The following day, July 10th, 2011, we made the climb. Hap had arranged for a vehicle to assist those who needed it. His son, Bill Scandrett Jr, a paramedic, was there if we needed him. Hap had special T-shirts made with the names of those twenty who were lost printed on the back. On a previous climb, Len Griffin had carried a small cross — draped with dog tags bearing each soldier's name. Len had planted it next to the mountain's benchmark. This time, we erected an American Flag that had flown over the Nation's Capital on the 20th of April, 2011. We all stood there at attention, saluted, and then mounted a plaque on a fence at the crest of the hill. After the climb, we stopped by the Stephens County Historical Society Currahee Military Museum. Colonel Tarleton donated a Currahee Flag to the museum's Vietnam Exhibit. The exhibit now contains the flag, cross, and the dog tags — donated on July 11th, 2010.

The following day, we bid farewell to Hap, our beloved leader and his beautiful and gracious wife, Barbara. We all headed home feeling much better than we had before arriving in Cumming, Georgia.

"Currahee," Brothers!

CHAPTER 17

Lost in Maine

Late at night, I roamed Portland's clubs in search of a good time. I was a pitiful sight. I stood stooped. My head hung as if I had committed some terrible crime. I didn't walk — I stumbled. At twenty-one, I was well on my way to becoming an alcoholic. I looked twice my age. I lived in an apartment at thirty-eight State Street in Portland. I slept during the day and stayed out all night. I spent my military disability pay on rent and booze. I was burning the candle at both ends. I was trying to capture the experiences I thought I missed while in the Army. I was emotionally numb. I picked up a lot of fast women. They meant nothing to me. I couldn't even remember their names the next day. They got angry with me and called me a bastard. I was.

After six months without work, I managed to land an interview at Mercy Hospital in Portland, Maine. My older brother worked there prior to medical school. Becoming a surgical technician in those days didn't require college. In 1970, candidates were hired off the street. They were trained by the hospital nurses and nuns. Working in the operating room wasn't for everyone. Few people wanted it. It took a special breed. Most people didn't make it past day one. The sight of blood made them nauseous. They fainted or fled the working interview as soon as the surgeon drew the blade. I had seen blood before — lots of it. At the end of the interview, I was the only candidate standing. The surgical mask hid the smell of liquor on my breath. I was hired. I began training the next day.

Back then, hospitals had defined caste systems. Employees didn't socialize outside of their class. Doctors were the Gods. Nuns talked to the Gods and were strict. The nurses were compliant — they bowed to both doctors and nuns. Technicians were peons. We didn't talk to the Gods. We weren't supposed to have conversations with the nurses. We were expected to keep our mouths shut unless asked a question. As I said, it was a caste system. It was strict. No one broke the rules and held their jobs. I didn't hold mine long. I broke the rules. I didn't care. Life was not worth living.

She was 19 and in her second year of nursing school. Her doe-like brown eyes were all I saw when she looked across the operating room table. They were framed by her surgical cap and mask. The rest of her face was a mystery. One look, and I was entranced. She was the most beautiful thing I had ever seen. For the second time in my life, I fell in love. I didn't even know her name.

Six months after I started work, Guy "Robbie" Maxwell also remained standing through his hospital interview. Rob encouraged me to ask Barbara for a date. I was reluctant. I wasn't like Rob. When he exited the Marine Corps, he was an attractive young man. Women found him irresistible. He had more nice girlfriends than anyone I ever met. His home phone was constantly ringing. He didn't have to call girls. The girls were calling him! I watched in wonder. Rob finally convinced me to call her. So, I found the phone number to the student nurses' dormitory. They stayed in quarters at the bottom of the Eastland Hotel in downtown Portland. I primed myself with booze to find the courage. When she came to the phone, I was surprised. She readily accepted my request for a date.

I saw the disappointment on her face the night I went to pick her up. I didn't get it at the time. She told me years later. There were two technicians that worked at Mercy who shared the same first name. She thought the other David had called her. Fortunately for me, I kept asking her out. She made excuses. I kept trying. It was looking grim until she became ill. When I found out that she was sick, I asked a friendly nurse permission to enter the section of the hospital that was kept private for employees. I brought flowers and a get-well card. It made a difference. Persistence pays off at times. We started dating on a regular basis. We fell in love. It changed my life. I had a reason to live. I let up on my drinking. I looked to the future.

Barbara's parents lived about 70 miles from Portland on a farm in Berwick. She didn't own a car and had to live on the ten dollars a month they gave her. They supplied the things she needed to survive, but that was it. She cooked her own meals. She made her own clothes. She rarely left the dorm. One weekend she needed to go home. I offered to give her a ride. She accepted but warned me not to expect a warm welcome. I had long hair and a beard. Her parents wouldn't approve.

Barbara's father was from Alabama. He had been a cook in the Navy and aspired to be a pilot. After a few years in the Navy, he started college. At the start of World War II, his college days were cut short. He had enough education to quality for flight training with the Army Air Corps and they took him. After training, he flew fighters in Europe. He flew Spitfires on a tour with the Brits. He had several victories and was shot down several times. He was shot down on his last flight and interned in Portugal until the end of the war. He met and married his wife, Jean, while in the Army Air Corps. She was an Army nurse and 100% Italian from Ohio. Frank Atkins retired as a lieutenant colonel after surviving several rifts that forced him to re-enter the Air Force as an enlisted man before being re-commissioned when the war in Korea erupted.

When I met Colonel Atkins, he was dressed in his favorite attire. He was barefoot. He had a rolled, brown paper grocery bag on his head. He wore a yellowing, white tee shirt and tattered, green military trousers that had been cut off just above the knees. When I dropped Barbara off, he told me with his southern drawl not to come back unless I cut my hair. I did. I kept going back. The family was fascinating. They lived in a well preserved two hundred-year-old cape cod on twenty-two acres of wooded farmland. The house was full of antiques. Most of the furniture was oak with just a light coat of linseed oil. They cooked on an old cast iron wood stove. They heated the house with a pot-bellied wood stove in the fireplace. Barbara's bedroom upstairs was unheated. She survived the below zero temperatures with bundles of clothing and an electric blanket. There were catfish in the pond behind their house. Her father made dandelion wine from the flowers in the yard. They ate vegetables from the garden that they tilled with the farm tractor that they kept in their big red barn. Barbara's family shopped at discount stores. They conserved everything including their well water. They washed dishes in no more than an inch of water in the sink. The dishes were from rummage sales. They shared the bath water. The eldest got to bathe first, others waited in turn.

Barbara had a strict upbringing. She wasn't allowed to play until she had learned something new in the kitchen. She knew how to cook and bake as well as sew. She baked apple pies from the apple trees in her front yard and pies from the berries in the woods behind the house. She made her clothes from patterns she cut from magazines with cloth they kept bundled in the attic. Barbara was a cheerleader at Berwick High School. She was in good shape and attractive. She hadn't dated much. Her parents didn't allow it. She felt out of place in Maine. She spent most of her life in Homestead, Florida. It was her father's last duty station. Her father retired in Maine and brought the family with him. Barbara felt displaced. She missed Florida. She wasn't used to the isolation of living in the country. She was shocked when the local boys arrived at school with manure on their barn boots. She wasn't used to the Maine accent. To her, it seemed strange and hickish.

It wasn't long before Barbara's father wanted to know my plans. What were my intentions? I had to make a decision. Well, not me actually. I knew that women chose the man, not the other way around. Barbara and I made plans. We decided to marry, leave Maine and head south. I knew she was marrying me just to get away from her strict parents. I didn't care. I would take her on any terms. I was in too deep. I applied for college at Memphis State University. It was a random choice. I was surprised when they accepted me. I hadn't been a good student in high school. I learned later that the college administrators thought the E's on my report card stood for excellent. With such high grades in Latin and other difficult courses, they accepted me immediately. Go figure.

I left for Memphis in January of 1972. I drove there in my yellow Ford Pinto. I stayed in the dormitory there with a Navy veteran who was a few years older. My first semester was difficult. I hadn't studied before and had to learn how. Somehow, I managed to pull a B average. I met my friend, Steve Jordan, there. He lived a few doors down the hall with his friend from Halls, Tennessee. We became friends and I went to his home on the weekends. It was culture shock to say the least. We had a great time that semester before I headed back to Maine. It was a good time for us both. It was a healing time for me. I needed it.

When Barbara and I married that summer, it was the happiest day of my life. I'm not so sure about her. She cried all night. Women. Who understands them? I drank the bottle of champagne by myself as she wept in the hotel bedroom. The next day, we headed to Memphis and left Maine in our rear-view mirror. Our new life together began. We are still together after more than 45 years. I'm pretty sure she has grown to like me.

CHAPTER 18

Steve Jordan

At first, he thought I was "uppity." I couldn't help it. The Army had stolen my smile. I tried to fit in. It was difficult. I reckon y'all can understand. I was only a few years older, but my experience in Vietnam had aged me. Steve said that I "wore my worry." He and his college dorm roommate, Ricky, still had their innocence. I wished I had mine too.

Steve talked funny. He referred to his father as his "Daddy." To his father's face, he called him, "Sir." He referred to and called his mother, "Mother" or "Mam." He always had "hankerings." He was always "fixin'" to do things. He called me a "Yankee." He asked me to "tote" things or to "carry" him somewhere. Places and things weren't close or far away. They were "near-about" or down "yonder."

On weekends, Steve "carried" me to his home in Halls, Tennessee. We drove in his VW station wagon or in my yellow Ford Pinto. We drove across iron bridges that spanned muddy rivers. We passed farmland with tenant farm houses surrounded by white cotton. In forested areas, kudzu coiled around the many species of trees — ash, boxelder, mulberry, beech, cottonwood and sweetgum. We drove through tiny towns with names like "Covington," "Henning," "Ripley," and "Gates." We passed white mansions with Roman columns. We stopped for fuel in towns where the gas stations had signs that read, "White Only," and "Colored."

Halls was surrounded by towns like "Dyersburg," "Nutbush," "Friendship," and "Fowlkes." The small town of Halls had a population of about two-thousand. It was clearly divided. Neat, middle class homes were on one side of town, and rows of white shanties and shacks on the other. The center of town had one main street. The buildings were mostly one story with a few two-story skyscrapers. People sat outside the bank, barbershop, clothing stores, and shoe shop. The men wore coveralls with suspenders over their white shirts, while they rocked in their rocking chairs. Women wore full length dresses and bonnets and looked like they were on their way to church.

Steve's home was modest in size and neat. The yard was well groomed and the house was surrounded by flowers. It had a fresh coat of white paint. Flower pots hung from the eves above the front porch. The house was filled with antiques. The furniture was oak with a coat of linseed oil that kept it fresh. The bedrooms had big brass beds with comforters and white hand-knit bedspreads.

His lovely mother waited on us and treated me like her son. His father was dressed in business attire and wanted to hear my background. He wasn't fond of the service. I don't think he was particularly fond of Yankees. He wasn't shy about it. When he disagreed with something I said, he would say, "That dog won't hunt." But, they treated us to home cooked meals. In the morning, we ate "grits," biscuits with gravy, and ham and eggs. In the afternoon we had "hush puppies" and ham sandwiches with our sweet tea. In the evening, they treated us to giant steaks as long as your forearm, okra, black-eyed peas, and collard greens.

Steve took me around town. He showed me where he went to high school and where he had been shot. He still had the pellets under the skin on his arm and hand. We walked under the dogwood trees and watched the locals playing baseball behind his house. It was a big event. There must have been twenty-five people there. He showed me where Jerry Lee Lewis played the piano in a small building near the house. I could picture the young girls swooning over the upcoming young star. He took me to his friends' houses. They lived on farmland. Their mothers canned peaches and pickles. They left berry pies on their window sills to cool. The boys drove pickup trucks, worked their family farms, raised hogs or tended farm animals. They kept jugs of white lightning that they hid from their mothers and drank from mason jars. They shot vermin at the dump.

We went to the secret swimming hole and the shack where the locals hung out. The girls were "purdy." They knew how to flirt and bat their eyes. They wore blue eye shadow and had long lashes. They twirled their hair and played hard to get. They joined sororities and learned how to dress in that southern belle style.

Before I left to drive back to Memphis State University, Steve's roommate and Ricky's family insisted that I fill my tank with their farm's fuel. As I pulled out of their dirt driveway, they stood together, waved and said, "Y'all come back, now!"

They were the salt of the earth and a breath of fresh air. I loved them all. I just wished I could show it with a smile. It was difficult to smile. As my best college friend, Steve Jordan, said: I "wore my worry."

CHAPTER 19

Saul Brown

He never remarried after Mildred. He lived alone in a one-bedroom duplex for thirty-seven years after she passed. Oh, he had plenty of opportunities. There were frequent female visitors. He just never took any of them seriously. After Mildred, he wasn't interested — none of them touched his heart. Women visitors always came as a group. They called themselves "Saul's Harem." Saul entertained them with his art, his music, and his dinner specialty — spaghetti and red wine. I think that's all he knew how to cook. I never knew him to make anything else — that was his world — art, music, women, spaghetti and wine. Barbara and I were let into his world by accident — literally. He fell off a truck-bed during one of his many photo-shoots for the paper. Barbara thought our eccentric neighbor might need a hot meal when he broke his leg. She made him something special — an apple pie — to go with a plate of her baked-chicken. We brought the meal over and rang his doorbell. He hobbled to the door on his crutches. Before he let us in, he swore us to secrecy. "Don't let anyone know what you see here," he said. We agreed. He was so secretive, I hoped he didn't have a body hidden somewhere. When we entered his home, I felt like I had just walked through the looking glass into wonderland. From the outside, it was just an ordinary house. But, on the inside it was magical. No one would suspect such wonderful things existed in such a humble abode.

Saul Theodore Brown was the son of Russian immigrants. He attended Tech High School in Memphis and graduated from the Memphis Academy of Fine Arts with a degree in Fine Art. He later endowed the University. There's an art scholarship in his name. Barbara and I met him when we first moved to Memphis. In 1972, I rented a one-bedroom duplex on a quiet street not far from Memphis State University for seventy dollars a month. It was a modest place, but clean and quiet. In the evenings, we heard classical music coming from the other half of our building. It was our neighbor. Saul was hard of hearing. He was fond of Mozart and played it loud. I didn't mind though. I enjoyed the change from my rock music. Saul introduced himself one day as we passed on our front steps. He was in his early-sixties, but he dressed and acted much younger. When we met, he had a black beret over his long, white hair. He wore a white pullover, a red scarf, blue jeans and long red and white striped stockings with his high-top, red sneakers with yellow laces. He was quite a sight when he rode his ten-speed bicycle in that outfit. I knew then that there was something different about him. He reminded me of a cross between an old hippie and "the cat in the hat." Saul was an artist — not by profession — by hobby. He was a photographer by trade — he worked for the Memphis Press-Scimitar as their chief photographer for twenty years. He was friendly enough; but prior to the accident, he kept to himself. When he met Barbara, though, his eyes lit up. He had an eye for beauty, as I did. I didn't mind. Men were always interested in Barbara. It was easy to see why. I liked that he saw what I saw. Plus, she was a great cook! Barbara and I took care of Saul for the six weeks he was laid up with his broken leg. Barbara cooked his meals. I ran errands. I painted his apartment. I mowed his lawn. One day, I mowed his name in the grass in the back yard. He got the biggest kick out of that. I still have the photos of him posing by his name in the lawn.

Saul kept stacks of boxes filled with photos in his attic. I saw the boxes through the chicken wire that separated our units when we first moved there. Each box was labeled by the date and place the photos were taken. He was a prolific photographer, and his photos were artistic — most in black and white. Saul was a frequent traveler. His travels took him all over the world. His photograph subjects included people from the many countries he visited. He shot everyone — from royalty to people on the street. It didn't matter. They all had something interesting about them. His apartment was covered in artworks and photographs of famous people like Elvis. Portraits adorned the apartment. There were many paintings — oil and watercolors — large and small. Every inch of his walls was covered. One evening, Saul shot Barbara and me in his living room after dinner. He used a small cheap camera and a pen-light for background lighting. I remember him telling me that it wasn't the camera that took the picture. He wanted to get a shot of my hair. He said, "Wait — one day you won't have any hair. You'll appreciate this." He was partially right. I have a bald spot now, and my hairline has receded.

Barbara and I had no idea that we were living next to someone famous. It wasn't until we read it in the paper that we discovered that Saul got the Freedom Foundation's award for photography the year we moved to Memphis. I got to know each one of his artworks intimately over time. I was a painter — not that kind of painter. I was painting houses while working my way through college. Our landlord saw me painting our duplex and hired me to paint all of the homes on our dead-end street. I painted Saul's home for free. It needed it. Saul had lived there as a bachelor for a long time after Mildred died. Like most bachelor's, he never paid much attention to cleaning. He was too busy painting portraits. I had to move each of his paintings before I could paint. Mildred's portrait had a place of honor in the center of his living room. He painted her wearing her nursing cap. He didn't talk much about Mildred. It was a sensitive subject for him. His eyes teared when I asked about the beautiful lady in the painting as I took it down. He said she was his wife who had died long ago. He never mentioned her again. Most of Saul's art was never shown to the public until after his death. Most art critics still don't recognize his works. He painted under an assumed name — Dorogoy. The art critics still don't know who the mystery artist — Dorogoy — was who painted those classic portraits on display on their website. Only those of us who knew him well knew. I have to laugh when I read their comments. Imagine — I know more than the Memphis art critics! Well, at least in this case.

Years after Barbara and I moved away, I flew into Memphis on one of my helicopter trips. I spent a few nights with Saul. Later, he came to visit us in Virginia. He stayed at our house for a few nights while roaming around Washington, DC during the day. I showed him our Presidential helicopters and some of the projects I was working on at the squadron. He really enjoyed himself, and we enjoyed having him. He took a lot of photos of our girls — Alicia and Merisa.

Saul called us shortly before he passed away. He never told us he was sick. But, when he said "goodbye," it had a finality to it. We realized when he hung up the phone that we would never see or hear from him again. It was a sad ending to a wonderful relationship. Our eccentric friend was gone. Saul passed away in Memphis on March 13, 1992 at the home of Myron Taylor, Mildred's brother. The Memphis library hosts his collection of photographs and paintings. They are also displayed on the library's website.

Remember when you see the "Dorogoy" signature, it's a painting by Saul. You'll be one up on the critics.

CHAPTER 20

Fastest Drinker at the Bar

All twenty of our legs — fourteen of them in blue Marine Corps trousers with red "blood stripes" — dangled over the bar. Several pairs of our shiny black corfam shoes — those belonging to the tallest among us — nearly touched the stools' seats below. My "leather neck" collar on my dress blues — adorned with its gold and silver globes and anchors — felt tight around my throat. I swallowed in anticipation. I made the mistake of examining the x-ray there on the wall. It was framed and hanging among the many squadron plaques and aviation pictures that were under the bar's brass bell. In hindsight, it was probably not a good idea to peek at that x-ray — at least not while sitting on the bar with that beer-stein in-hand. The x-ray was a sobering sight. One of Whiting Field's flight surgeons hung it there. It served as a warning about the danger associated with the ritual we were about to undertake. It was an x-ray of someone's stomach with his metal naval aviator wings inside. Some unfortunate flight-training graduate had been rushed to surgery from the Officer's Club the day that x-ray was taken. The pins on the back of those wings could be clearly seen. It must have hurt like hell as those wings went down his throat.

The winging ceremony had gone well. As I stood there in the chapel at Whiting Field, Barbara was at my side with our eleven-month-old daughter, Alicia, in her arms. Barbara and a Navy Captain — a four striper — pinned the new gold wings of a Naval Aviator on my chest. After shaking the Captain's hand, I rejoined the other newly-minted naval helicopter pilots on the chapel's stage for our group graduation picture. There were ten of us graduating that day in February of 1977 — seven Marine Corps 2nd Lieutenants, one Navy Ensign, one Iranian Midshipman, and one Coast Guard Ensign. After the pictures were taken, we adjourned to the Officer's Club. Barbara and Alicia went home —

no wives or children were allowed in the club until after happy hour. It was a naval tradition. I'm sure that it's a tradition that no longer exists. Things have changed. Naval aviation is no longer a "man's world."

It took a little more than a year for me to complete flight training. It had been a hard year. It began with API — Aviation Preflight Indoctrination — four weeks of ground school academics and water survival training in Pensacola, followed by fixed-wing training at Saufley Field. It finished with us flying helicopters at Whiting Field in Milton, Florida. Because I studied Physics at Memphis State University, API — except for water survival training — seemed pretty easy to me. At API, we studied aerodynamics, aircraft engines and systems, meteorology, air navigation and FAA rules and regulations. For me, it was "too easy," as it turned out. When I started "primary" — fixed-wing flight training — at Saufley, my flight instructor, a Marine "hard-ass," looked at my API grades and decided to make my life difficult. "No Marine scores that high in API academics," he told me. "You must have cheated. I'm going to wash you out!" After our first flight, he promised to give me a "down" — a failing grade — on my second flight. He didn't. He waited until my third flight, so he could have a little more time to toy with the 2nd Lieutenant with the highest API academic average.

When a student gets a "down" during "Primary," the Navy gives "him" — or "her" these days — a break. They transfer the student to a different instructor. When I reported to my new flight instructor, he was on duty behind the VT-1 Operations Duty Officer's desk. ODO was one of the instructors' additional duties when they weren't flying. The ODO was responsible for controlling and monitoring all of the squadron's flight operations by radio. Captain Fred "Assassin" McCorkle — a native of Harriman, Tennessee, and a graduate of East Tennessee State University — was an intimidating figure. Although he wasn't a very tall man, he was ruggedly built and maintained a serious poker-face. The corners of his upper lip turned down in a slight scowl, which I later learned was his natural way of smiling. It made him look like "Chesty" Puller — one of the Corps' legends. Captain McCorkle was a former Vietnam War helicopter pilot with fifteen-hundred combat flight hours. Assassin's uniform was adorned with a stack of multi-colored ribbons — including a Distinguished Flying Cross with Gold Star, a Purple Heart, Air Medals with seventy-six Strike/Flight awards, and numerous other "decorations" for valor. Holding a radio handset in each hand, he looked at me and said, "I don't give downs, Lieutenant. You'll DOR." DOR was the acronym for "drop on request." As in Seal training, where dropouts ring the bell to quit, all we had to say was, "I want to DOR," and the "pain" would be over — we would be out of Navy flight training. Obviously, I wasn't having fun. To complicate matters, Barbara had given birth to Alicia at the end of Ground School — so, my home life had been turned upside down. But, I decided then and there that I wasn't going to quit — they would have to force me out.

Assassin pulled the T-34B Mentor's control stick aft, and the red and white, tandem seat, single-propeller aircraft began a steep climb through a hole in the clouds. I was pinned to my parachute and the back of the front seat by the G-forces. My face became heavy and contorted. I squeezed the muscles in my calves as hard as possible to keep the blood from draining from my head and blacking out. After leveling off at five-thousand feet, we flew peacefully above the cloud cover until Assassin found another opening in the clouds. Assassin then dipped the aircraft's left wing down and asked, "What's the name of that field below us?" I remained silent — trying to figure out where the hell we were and trying to remember the airfield's name from the previous night's homework. When I hesitated to answer, the aircraft rolled left, became inverted, and began a steep dive. As I hung upside down in the straps, I could see the airfield below growing in size. We kept diving. Suddenly, I could see the name that was painted on the intersection of the airfield's runway grow bigger and bigger. Finally, I blurted out, "Holley Field!" As I did, the aircraft pulled into a steep, rolling climb; I was once again pinned to my seat. So, that's how it began — eleven flights of intensive training with no excuses accepted for not knowing the answers to Assassin's never-ending questions. And, so it continued, with touch-and-goes, slow-flight, approach-turn stalls, spins and his endless grilling over emergency procedures. At the end of each flight, we debriefed; I stood in a cold sweat, while he went over every detail of my performance. Every day was a challenge. Every day I wondered if I would make it. It took all I had to hang on. At some point, I realized that all I had to do was continue to hang on, not quit, and I could make it. I might not make astronaut, but I could make it. I could get those wings of gold. Assassin was a man of his word — he didn't give downs — he just scared the ever-living-shit out of you!

I'll never forget the day that Captain McCorkle climbed out of the back seat of that T-34B. We were at an outlying field practicing touch-and-goes. After a number of them, Captain McCorkle said, "Make the next one a full stop." After the aircraft rolled out and came to a stop, the canopy above me slid aft and opened. As he unstrapped and began to jump on the starboard wing, he said, "Take it around three times, and come back and get me." Just like that, the Assassin was gone, and I was on my own. The Primary "off-wing" flight — a check flight by another instructor — was probably the easiest flight of my training. Captain McCorkle had grilled me so well, that I had the answers before the questions left the lips of the Navy Instructor Pilot. I came back from that flight with my first above average grades —Assassin rarely gave above averages. My next flight was a "solo!"

After a student aviator "solos," they have a "tie-cutting ceremony" at the Officer's Club. Tie-cutting is a tradition in all of aviation — civilian and military. During the tie-cutting ceremony, the instructor pilots cut the neckties off the students, symbolizing the cutting of the ties to — and dependence of the students on — their instructors. It means that the students are finally capable of taking off, flying, and landing on their own without killing themselves. I was the only Marine student at my tie-cutting. The rest were Navy or Coast Guard students. When the time came for the instructors to cut the ties, we students all lined up for the ceremony. After a brief speech by the head instructor, the ties were cut. The Navy instructors had scissors and snipped their students' ties off — but not the "Assassin." Captain McCorkle pulled a huge Bowie knife from its sheath and said, "You better turn your head, Lieutenant Libbey, if you want to keep your nose." I turned my head. I felt my tie being pulled forward, and with one giant swing and swoop of the knife, my tie was cut just below the knot. Assassin gave me one of his "upside down" smiles as he handed me my tie. As an aside, "Assassin" went on to become a three-star General before he retired. Lieutenant General Frederick McCorkle became the number one aviator in the Marine Corps — the Deputy Commandant for Aviation.

After flying the T-34B, we students stepped up to flying the North American T-28 Trojan. The T-28 was a much larger, 1950's era trainer with a huge, nine-cylinder, radial-engine. The T-28 was used by the Air Force, Navy and Marine Corps for flight training. It had also been used as a light-attack aircraft during the Vietnam War. It was loud, relatively fast for a prop, and well-suited for aerobatics. We learned formation flying, aerobatics, and instrument flying in the T-28B. That's the aircraft where we received our first instrument rating. Flying the T-28 on instruments required that we wear an oxygen mask. I hated that. It had a positive-pressure, oxygen system. That meant that when you opened your mouth, oxygen was going to be forced into your lungs, whether you wanted it or not. It took some getting used to. After flying the T-28, the Navy decided that I was more suited for flying helicopters than jets. They sent me to Whiting Field to train in helicopters. I was thrilled. I hadn't cared for flying with an oxygen mask all that much; and I had heard stories about how much fun it was to be flying low and slow in helicopters. They said that you could see everything through the chin bubbles; and you weren't pulling G's all the time. I've got to tip my hat to the jet guys, though. Pulling G's all the time is a lot of work! It wears you out. I can't see how it could be all that much fun. But, then again, jet jocks get to shoot their watches down while dogfighting with their knife hands at the club. It's impressive!

So, after learning to fly the T-28, I was off to HT-8 at Whiting Field for helicopter flight training in Milton. Flying helicopters is fun — particularly in the little TH-57 Bell Jet Ranger. Once you master hovering — the hardest part of flying helicopters — it's a blast. When students are learning to hover, they start in a huge field — several football fields in size. The instructor teaches you to fly by allowing you to operate one control at a time. In forward flight, the "cyclic stick" controls direction — fore, aft, or side to side. The "collective stick" controls the power and the "pitch" of the rotor blades. You pull up to add power and increase pitch. You push down to reduce power and pitch. The pitch of the rotor blade determines its bite of the air and how fast you are going to go. In a hover, foot-pedals control rotational direction by the pitch on the tail rotor. The tail rotor counteracts the torque created by the spinning main rotor blades and helps keep the aircraft in balanced flight. Without a tail rotor, the helicopter's fuselage would spin in the opposite direction that the main rotors are spinning, because of the main rotors' torque. Without getting into a lot of aerodynamics, let's just say that learning to hover is a humbling experience. If you can keep the helicopter in that huge field the first time you attempt it without spinning or crashing, you're doing pretty damn good. It's funny watching newbies go up and down, spinning and sliding all over the field the first time they attempt hovering. Once you master it though, there's nothing like it. You can fly forward, backwards, side-ways, or just stay still in a hover. You can turn on a dime in a hover, and then dart off in any direction. As the old saying goes, "To fly is heavenly — to hover is divine."

Well, there's a lot more training involved in learning to fly helicopters — square patterns, auto-rotations, cut-guns, etc. But it's all fun. Once I completed flying the TH-57, I moved on to HT-18 and the final phase of Navy flight training. At HT-18 we learned to fly the TH-1L and UH-1 "Huey." The Huey is that infamous helicopter you see flying in massive formations in the Ken Burns series on Vietnam. After flying the little TH-57, the Huey seems huge. It's not really. Not when you compare it to the Marine Corps huge CH-53E, the largest helicopter in the Navy and Marine Corps. I think the CH-53E is still the largest helicopter in the Western World, although the new CH-53K that's still in development is even larger.

Anyway, that brings us back to the Whiting Officer's Club, where I was sitting on the bar with nine other graduates. Per tradition, the bartender had filled our steins with a mixture of booze from the bottles in the bar-well — he used the cheap stuff — the stuff few people want to drink. It looked awful and smelled bad too. The initiation ceremony called for us — on command — to chug that drink as fast as we could and catch our new wings of gold from the bottom of the stein in our teeth. The first one to slam his empty stein on the bar while keeping his wings between his teeth would be declared the winner and the "Fastest Drinker at the Bar." The winner got to keep a beautiful stein with the HT-18 logo and "Fastest Drinker at the Bar" engraved above gold Naval Aviator Wings. Well, I made a huge mistake. At the start, the Lead Instructor gave us the go ahead, "One, two three, go!" I threw my head back, chugged that awful stuff in one huge gulp, caught the wings in my teeth, and slammed my stein on the bar. I thought I had won. But, not so fast. Our big Coast Guard student had tied me — or so they said. Given that there was a tie, the instructors told us that there needed to be a run-off. Like an idiot, I nodded my head in agreement. The bartender refilled our steins with another obnoxious and odious concoction from the bar-well. And, this is where I made the fatal mistake of peeking at that x-Ray under the bar's bell. It must have been on my mind, because when the order to go was given, I tilted my head back, opened my throat, poured that junk down my throat, and nearly fell backwards off the bar. The Coastie got the stein and the title of "Fastest Drinker at the Bar."

That night as I hugged the commode, I held my new gold Naval Aviator's wings in my clenched fist. Life was good!

CHAPTER 21

Libbo Email

Several weeks ago, I received an email from an old friend. It read, "Libbo, a belated happy birthday to you, shipmate. Hope all is well. Recently saw the attached at the USMC museum. Aloha and Semper Fi, Rooster." That short note wouldn't mean much to most people, but it did to me and would to those of us who served together in the Marine Corps. It was poetic, containing a lot of hidden meaning and an attached picture. This short email brought back a lot of memories of my time in the Corps.

Marines are always hanging labels on people and things. Once you are labeled, it sticks forever. "Libbo" is a word Marines use for liberty — time off without having to take leave. "Libbo" was also the call-sign given to me by my squadron mates sometime during the 80's, when I was stationed in Kaneohe Bay, Hawaii. It was a clever twist on my last name, "Libbey," and a reminder of a long-ago liberty incident, which is another story that I won't get into. So, seeing "Libbo" written again after so many years, put me back in the action, if only for a moment.

The birthday greeting was intended to let me know that Greg "Rooster" Reuss hadn't forgotten our friendship. "Shipmate" referred to us as having shared the same stateroom aboard the USS New Orleans for six months during a Western Pacific deployment. The USS New Orleans was an amphibious assault ship named after the Battle of New Orleans during the War of 1812. It was commissioned in 1968, and eventually used for target practice and sunk off the coast of Kauai. While aboard, Rooster and I were quartered with two other pilots, Clark Leevy from Dallas, Texas, and Bill "Button" Tarbutton from the Eastern Shore of Maryland. It was my third six-month deployment while in the Marine Corps. I completed two deployments in the Mediterranean and two in the Western Pacific. On this deployment, we sailed all over the

Pacific from Hawaii to Guam, the Philippines, Korea, Singapore, Australia, Thailand, and more.

The attachment in the email is this picture of us CH-53D pilots standing in front of one of our aircraft assigned to HMM-265. CH-53D aircraft are heavy-lift transport helicopters that were used by the United States Marine Corps from 1966 until 2012. The US Air Force, German and Mexican Air Forces also flew them. Today, they can only be found in aircraft museums or on pedestals in front of military bases. I had logged about three-thousand hours in the CH-53D by the time I retired from the Corps in 1994.

I have fond memories of most of the pilots in this photo. I can't remember all of them, however. Time has added some cob webs. I'm surprised that somehow this photo found its way into the National Museum of the Marine Corps. That museum, erected near Marine Corps Base, Quantico, Virginia in 2006, is a revered place for us Marines. It contains priceless military artifacts and tells the stories of the legends who have served since the founding of the Marine Corps on November 10th, 1775, through today's current events in Afghanistan and Iraq. It's special to have a picture of us there, average Marines standing among such giants.

Kneeling in the left front is Clark Leevy. Not long after this photo was taken, Clark left active duty and joined the Marine Corps reserves. Now he is a Captain flying B747's for American Airlines. I'm sure that he will be forced to retire soon. I see him on LinkedIn every now and then. Fly safe, Clark!

Kneeling to the right is Steve "Blow" Dreyer. Steve, a former embassy guard in Vietnam, couldn't get augmented in the Marine Corps, so he joined the Air Force. He retired as a full Colonel and is the Director for Operations in Bucharest at United States Air Forces, Europe. Well done, Blow!

Standing on the left is Jordan Yankov. As a Major, Jordan taught tactics at Marine Corps Aviation and Weapons Tactics Squadron One in Yuma, Arizona. He later became the Executive Officer of a helicopter squadron on the east coast. Jordan died in a helicopter mishap with three other Marines on the 8th of February 1992. He left behind his wife, Margaret, and their two children,

Katherine and Nikolas. His was the last funeral I agreed to attend. I miss his cocky grinning face.

To the right of Jordan is Bill "Button" Tarbutton. Before retiring as a Lieutenant Colonel, Button was a Presidential Command Pilot for the White House. Later, he was the Air Mission Commander who flew the lead aircraft during the rescue of Air Force Captain Scott O'Grady. O'Grady had been shot down by the Bosnian-Serb Army while flying his F-16C over Serb held Bosnia. Leading a flight of four helicopters and two AV-8 Harriers, Button flew into hostile Serb territory, grabbed O'Grady from under the nose of hostile Serb forces, and evaded surface to air missiles on the way back to the USS Kearsarge. After twenty years in the Marine Corps and a tour as a Squadron Commander, Button flew and maintained civilian medevac helicopters before retiring to his farm in Maryland. He likes the hunting and fishing there.

Standing tall and smiling in the center is Greg "Rooster" Reuss. Rooster, the author of the email, is a Naval Academy graduate who blew both of his knees out playing basketball for the Navy. Always a comedian, Rooster kept our spirits high during the long months at sea. Rooster stayed in the Corps for thirty years, attaining the rank of full Colonel. He eventually commanded Marine Aircraft Group 24. Aloha, Rooster!

To the right of Rooster is David Eames. I lost track of David after this deployment. I hope he is well.

Next to David is Dan Seifert. Dan transitioned to fixed-wing aircraft after this deployment and flew EA-6B aircraft for the Corps before retiring. He started his own business supporting war fighters after his stint in the Corps. Dan passed away from natural causes at the age of fifty-eight in 2014. He is sorely missed.

I'm on the far right. I retired after nearly twenty years in the Marine Corps, flying for the White House and commanding a training squadron of five-hundred Marines, HMT-302. After that, I managed Longshoremen, loading ships in Long Beach, California for twelve years before going back to the Marine Corps as a contractor in 2006. I left the Marine Corps for the final time in October of 2015. Being with the Marines was the best part of my working life. I miss my friends. Semper Fi, shipmates!

CHAPTER 22

Mark and Ted

The CH-53D was the western world's largest and most powerful helicopter at the time. It was a beast. It was the heavy-lift backbone of the Marine Corps. It carried thirty fully loaded combat Marines plus its crew. It hauled two fully loaded jeeps with trailers and drivers. It supported ten-thousand pounds on its external hook. The helicopter lifted Marine Corps artillery pieces. It was capable of recovering other helicopters if necessary. It was also a maintenance nightmare. Every hour spent in the air required a minimum of ten hours of maintenance on the ground. Marines called it the "shitter."

At twenty-two, he had one of the most difficult and challenging jobs in the Marine Corps. He was a CH-53D helicopter crew chief. Mark Stanley was a Cornhusker — a Nebraskan. He was exactly who the Marine Corps wanted. He loved the outdoors. He loved to hunt and fish. He loved machines. He was a gifted mechanic. Stanley was a natural. Knuckle-busting was nothing new to him. He relished it. He loved hot rods and muscle cars. He loved to turn wrenches on his Camaro. Bringing old cars back to life was a challenge. He couldn't get enough. He was the perfect person to keep a "shitter" flying.

Ted Dingas had a cherubic face — almost angelic. If he hadn't been forced to shave, it would have been covered in peach fuzz. A Texan not yet out of his teens, he was quick to learn and sharp-witted. He told stories. He was fast with one-liner comebacks. He joked about himself. He didn't mind being called a "first rag" — his Marine friends' term for first mechanic. Ted admired Mark Stanley. Stanley was like his big brother. Ted watched Mark's every turn of the wrench, and Mark guided Ted's every move. Ted knew that if he learned enough from Mark, one day he too would be a crew chief. Mark showed Ted as much as he could absorb.

Ted wouldn't become a crew chief overnight. It took years. There was a vast amount to learn.

The "shitter" was complex. It had many "systems" — engine, electrical, hydraulic, fuel, airframe and cargo handling. Systems went on and on. Mark learned them all. He knew every nut and bolt. He heard every sound. He knew every limitation. He knew when something was wrong before the pilots knew it. The pilots might fly the aircraft, but the crew chief owned it. Mark owned it. Pilots came and went. They walked off the aircraft after a flight — but not the crew chief — not Mark. He stayed with the aircraft all day until nightfall. Often, he would work on the aircraft in the darkness, preparing it for the next day's flight. Many times, it was his bedroom. He slept on the bench passenger seats. He moved about without a flashlight to avoid breaking the ship's light discipline. As I told you, Mark was the perfect crew chief — exactly who the Corps wanted.

When it happened, we were flying off the USS Guam — a helicopter aircraft carrier. Our squadron, HMM-264, was participating in an amphibious exercise with Spaniards near the town of Carboneras on the southern coast of Spain. Carboneras was an old town surrounded by mountainous, high desert. You may have seen the area if you ever watched spaghetti westerns. Clint Eastwood starred in the classic film, *"For a Few Dollars More,"* there. Some of the pilots flying our smaller helicopters discovered the movie set during the amphibious operation. The pilots landed and walked the set. They took pictures of themselves clowning around in the old west. Mark's aircraft was much too big to land there. It would blow the town away with its hurricane force-like winds.

Machines suffer from fatigue. When metal is subjected to repeated loading and unloading it loses its composition. Microscopic cracks form and it weakens. Like a coat hanger that has been bent repeatedly, it will eventually snap. Men also suffer from fatigue. When stressed repeatedly, they tire. When they tire, they make mistakes. They overlook things. In aviation, little things can kill you.

Mark's helicopter had a flaw in the design that related to the opening and closing of the aircraft's ramp door. The hooks and rollers that held the ramp door in place had worn after years and years of use. The ramp door kept falling down, so tired aircrews used safety wire to hold the door in place. When the ramp opened or closed, the ramp door's hydraulic actuator attempted to open and close the door. With the door held in place by safety wire, there was nowhere for the hydraulic pressure to go but up. The door's hydraulic actuator was located on the fuselage overhead just underneath the tail rotor drive shaft. The repeated pressure on the overhead caused the airframe to fatigue. On the 20th day of March 1978, it fractured while the aircraft was in flight. The actuator broke through the fuselage and into the spinning drive shaft. It acted like a lathe. The drive shaft was cut in half. With the driveshaft cut in half, the tail rotor stopped turning. The aircraft spun out of control without a tail rotor to counteract the torque from the main rotor blades. The pilot had no choice but to crash land while the helicopter was still upright.

Often, military men have premonitions of death. During the battle of Cold Harbor during the Civil War, Union soldiers were so certain of their impending death that they pinned their names or notes to loved ones on the back of their shirts. We weren't in combat or in the Civil War. Mark Stanley wasn't a Union soldier. He was a United States Marine. But, Mark had a premonition the night before he died. I know. I know, because he told me on the evening of March 19th. He was working on his aircraft on the ship's flight deck, as was Ted Dingas. Mark said, "Sir, I have a bad feeling. I think that if the operational tempo continues, someone will get hurt. Someone will die." I tried to alleviate his fears. I doubt it helped much. I was a lieutenant. I was a copilot. I didn't have the tools in my toolbox or the horsepower to make a difference. There wasn't a thing I could do to slow things down.

It wasn't the operational tempo that killed Mark Stanley, Ted Dingas or the three other infantry Marines who happened to be the unlucky passengers that day. It was a design flaw, metal fatigue and a mistake. Only the pilots would survive. The aircraft commander,

Major May, would spend months in the hospital. The copilot, Lieutenant Tim Dusenbury, would survive but would never be the same. He died in a mishap on the next deployment while on a joy ride with Lieutenant Steve Young in a Cobra helicopter. They flew into a cable stretched between mountain tops in Greece.

A few days after the crash, stunned Marines stood in formation on the flight deck of the USS Guam. Marines fired volleys from their M-16's into the air and out to sea. Then, it was time for the squadron's Marines to get back to work. The helicopters wouldn't fix themselves.

CHAPTER 23

Steve and Dues

There was silence on board after the tragedy. No one spoke. No one wanted to be the first to talk about it. The ship was like a church — no voices — no music — only the sounds of the creaking vessel as it rocked and pitched over the waves. It let me think. I got lost in my thoughts. All I could hear were their voices in my head. When he broke the silence, I was startled. He was angry. I had never seen Bob that way. I couldn't fault him. I was angry too — but more heartbroken than anything. I was numb. I wondered if this was ever going to end. I wondered if this was my destiny — to live with a broken heart.

Being at sea for six months can get lonely. It helps to have friends. My roommates, Bob and Kevin, were good friends. We got along well. You get to know someone when you live in close quarters. They were good people. Bob was much more experienced than Kevin and me. He had been a pilot for a long time. He had seen a lot of this stuff. But, you never really get used to it. He still wasn't used to it.

Bob pointed to the twisted remains of a helicopter on the hangar deck. He was disgusted. The pilots had been on a joy ride. They flew the aircraft into wires that were strung across mountaintops in Strimonikis, Greece. They were dead before they hit the ground. "They ought to make every pilot in the Marine Corps look at this shit!" he said. I hung my head. I was the personal effects officer. I was holding a plastic bag with the personal effects of the two pilots. Someone needed to clean the blood and fluids off their watches and wallets. Their belongings needed to be sent home to the families. I didn't want their wives to see what I saw. When the families asked for their effects, there should be no trace left. I wanted them to be clean. Someone had to do it. It might as well be me. I would make sure that the job was done right. I always did.

Steve Young was a lieutenant and a Marine cobra pilot in his early twenties. He was a single military-brat. His father was an Air Force General stationed in Europe. Steve lived in bases all over the United States and Europe. Steve had just made aircraft commander and was eager to impress his seniors. Tim "Dues" Dusenbury was a Marine CH-53D copilot from Florence, South Carolina. He and his wife, Nancy, had two sons, Timothy and William. On a previous deployment, he had been involved in an aircraft mishap. The crash took the lives of five Marines and put the pilot, Major May, in the hospital for months. Tim was never the same. He never recovered mentally. He wasn't ready to be an aircraft commander. He was skittish. He was still too jumpy. He panicked under pressure. His best friend, Fletcher "Fletch" Ferguson, was a Marine Captain and CH-46 aircraft commander. He was married and also from South Carolina — Abbeville.

Steve, Dues, Fletch, and I were playing cards a couple of nights before the accident. It was a nightly ritual. It helped pass the many months at sea. We would spread a green military blanket over a footlocker and squat next to the beds in Fletcher's stateroom. Fletch kept a huge tin of jalapeno peppers next to his locker. I don't know where he got it. It was the kind they use in restaurants. We got a kick out of watching each other try to swallow as many peppers as we could without having to stop. We paid the price the next day. Those peppers burned on the way out as much as they did going down.

Dues and Fletch went to a military academy together — the Citadel. They were always partners at cards. They cheated. We all knew it. We were only playing hearts. Whenever one of them wanted the other to discard a low card, he would break out singing, "Swing low sweet chariot." If they wanted to get rid of a high card, they would sing, "Fly me to the moon." Their hand gestures were hilarious. I wish I had it on video.

When Steve and Dues were killed on the 12th of August 1979, the card games stopped. It wouldn't be the same. It would be disrespectful. The cards were thrown away — the peppers too. Fletch had the stateroom to himself. Our friends were gone. He just heard the creaking of the vessel as it rocked and pitched over the waves. There were still months ahead for him to think of his missing friends. I had Bob and Kevin.

CHAPTER 24

Touchdown Johnston

This is no shit. There we were, engines burning and rotors turning on spot seven of the USS Iwo Jima, waiting for our lead, Ronnie "Touchdown" Johnston, to land on spot five. My hands tightened on the controls and my body tensed as Ronnie's aircraft made its approach to the side of the ship. This was always the exciting part — there wasn't much clearance between aircraft on those LPH ships. Only a few feet separated us from certain doom if he drifted too far aft. His intended landing point, Spot five, was just in front of us. His tail rotor would be right in our face when he set down. The Landing-Signal Man was guiding him into the spot, and sailors were standing by waiting to chock his wheels and chain his helicopter to the deck.

Just as Touchdown's copilot, Mark Meyers, yawed the big aircraft left, aligning it parallel to the ship and began his final hovering descent, the aircraft rolled to port away from the deck. It descended fifty feet and settled in the water below. Before I could start our Auxiliary Power Unit and shut down our CH-53D's turboshaft jet engines, Touchdown's aircraft began to sink. It rolled left, and the huge rotor blades beat the water violently as it went down under the waves, sinking tail first. Water flew everywhere; and as it slipped below the surface with all passengers, crew and cargo on board, the rotor blades were still turning — beating and churning the sea around them. Broken pieces of blades flew through the air and fell back to the ocean.

I'm not sure how I ended up on the deck before Ronnie; but there I was — sitting on spot seven, watching my friends in one of our beloved big iron helicopters slip below the surface of the Mediterranean off the coast of Turkey. Ronnie was a second tour aviator then and a few years senior to me. Because the ink on my Helicopter Aircraft Commander (HAC) designation papers was barely dry, he was the section leader. Under most circumstances, the lead aircraft would have landed before me. All I can figure is that he must have given me the lead, so he could let his copilot get some practice flying formation on my aircraft. It's hard to remember all the details after thirty-eight years! It was October of 1979.

Touchdown was an easy going, North Carolinian from Greenville and a graduate of East Carolina University. I always enjoyed flying copilot with him, although he could easily put you in your place with his dry sense of humor. He would make comments like, "We might all be a little more comfortable if you centered that ball," or "Bubba, can you add a little right stick, we're left wing down, and I'm getting the leans," or "Do you always prefer this side of the runway?" Watching him and the others go in the water was unnerving to say the least!

When it happened, we were off the coast of Saros Bay, Turkey assigned to HMM-264, participating in a very large amphibious exercise. We were part of the 34th Marine Amphibious Unit during exercise "Display Determination." There were dozens of ships positioned offshore with Marines and their cargo loading back from the beach — some by sea and some by helicopter. Ronnie's aircraft and mine were both full — packed with jeeps, trailers, and a few Marines with all their gear. There were thousands of Marines ashore, and it would take us all day to get the Marines back on their ships.

When an aircraft goes down, the ship's controllers know how many people are on board. Crossing the shoreline, we always made the radio call, such as, "Leroy thirty-three, flight of two, feet wet, Angels one, with seven souls, and Leroy thirty-five with five souls, fuel state one point zero." That let the controllers know that we were inbound at one thousand feet and gave the number of people on each aircraft and how much fuel in hours and minutes was remaining. So, we knew how many people were in that aircraft as it began its descent to the bottom of Saros Bay. Fortunately for everyone, the ship was at rest rather than steaming. If it had been underway, the ending to this story would be entirely different!

After shutting down my aircraft's engines and applying the rotor brake, I unstrapped my harness, disconnected my intercom from my helmet, and jumped out of the seat. I hurried outside. Marines and sailors were scurrying about the deck. The ship's siren blared, as a voice on the 1MC announced, "Man-overboard, Port; Now set the sea-rescue detail!" All eyes were on the port side of the ship, watching the bubbling water and debris pop to the surface.

We Naval Aviators had all been through water survival training in Pensacola, Florida before we were ever allowed to go near an aircraft. Navy water survival training is a grueling course, and among other things, we were taught how to escape a helicopter while it's upside down in the water. However, there's a big difference between escaping from an empty barrel submerged in the sterile environment of a pool than escaping from a fully loaded helicopter on its way to the bottom of the ocean! All that stuff that Marines load on your aircraft — the trailers loaded with camouflage netting, sleeping bags, tents, rifles, helmets and personal items — it all becomes a tangled mess waiting to entangle your arms and legs while you thrash around, searching for a way out in the darkness.

As we waited there on deck, fixated on the bubbles and debris, I felt my heart sink with them. We had already lost two friends on this six-month deployment when they flew into some wires strung between mountain tops in Greece. On the previous deployment, we had lost five Marines, including two great aircrew members. This couldn't be happening again! I was helpless, an observer in another bad dream.

It wasn't long before the ship's crew had a boat in the water, and sailors were making their way to the debris field. Then, after what seemed like an eternity, a Marine burst up through the surface and gasped for air! And then another! And another! I started counting. One by one, they popped to the surface, each one grasping at the air and gasping for breath. Finally, the seventh and last Marine broke through the surface. They were all alive! I must have been holding my breath, because I took in a huge breath of air, and I felt like I too had finally breached the surface! Some of those in the water remembered to inflate their survival vests, and others continued to tread water until Sailors hauled them out of the sea into their boat. After the last Marine was back on board and the ship's boat was recovered, we strapped back into our helicopter on spot 7, cranked up, took off, and resumed flying. Only, this time we were a flight of one. There were still lots of Marines on the beach who had to get back to their home away from home at sea.

The Aircraft Mishap Investigation Board eventually recovered enough of the aircraft to determine the cause of the mishap. One of the drive shafts from an engine to the main transmission had failed, leaving the helicopter without enough power or lift to stay airborne. Ronnie had taken the controls and saved his crew and passengers from certain death by preventing the helicopter's rotors from impacting the ship. Although underpowered, he had managed to slide the aircraft away from the ship and land it gently in the water. "Touchdown" Johnston is still around, and I'm sure if he's still flying, he's telling someone, "You're a little left wing down, Bubba!" I hope all of his landings are good ones!

CHAPTER 25

Hawaii

It was always the first island we flew by on our way to the Big Island. It was a short flight — only sixty-six miles or so to the east of the Kaneohe Marine Corps Air Station on the windward shore of Oahu. I marveled at the northern shore of Molokai. The island has magnificent cliffs on its northern shore. The "Pali" rises more than twenty-five hundred feet from the ocean's surface. The island flattens out somewhat at the top, but it's still rolling mountainous terrain. Our squadron, HMH-463, lost a helicopter there just weeks before I checked onboard. The pilots had overestimated their ability and underestimated the danger of flying in mountainous terrain. The families of those lost were still reeling from the loss of life.

About half way along the northern length of Molokai, we passed a small peninsula that juts out into the ocean. The peninsula is flat and has a small runway that we used for night training. The lack of lights in the surrounding area provided a perfect environment for the use of night vision devices. The only life on the peninsula was at the leper colony of Kalaupapa — a colony established by Father Damien in the nineteenth century. I could envision the lepers being forced to jump from the Warwick — a wooden schooner — in 1866. The ship's crew threw supplies over the side and returned back to Oahu. The patients had to fend for themselves. Many drowned. Those who survived were left isolated there for their entire lives. Initially, they lived in caves or fashioned shelter from sticks and shrub. More than eight-thousand patients were forced to live there over the years. There were still a few lepers living at Kalaupapa the last time I visited. They were the few descendants of those who managed to make it to the rocky shore. Today, muleskinners ferry tourists from the top of the island down the steep cliffs' switchbacks to visit and have lunch with the "survivors." People are warned not to stare or ask too many stupid questions. Father Damien's church is in Kalaupapa. It's a popular tourist attraction for those who prefer offbeat vacations. As we flew east, we saw the magnificent waterfalls and inlets that few people in the world have experienced. Molokai was my favorite island. On Molokai, there are more than 250 species of Hawaiian plants — most are unique to Hawaii. Rare birds are also visible if one looks carefully. I think Molokai was one of Barbara's favorites. She still has her muleskinner's certificate from riding down the cliffs to the colony. She goes for the less traditional kinds of vacations. I guess that's one reason why we get along so well.

Maui is just east of Molokai — at 120 Knots, it was another short flight in our CH-53D helicopter. Just about every experienced traveler has been to Maui. But, I'll bet only a handful have tasted the deep-dish apple pie at the Kahului airport. It's to die for. In the 80's, our aircraft only carried two hours of fuel. We had to refuel at Maui. We couldn't make it all the way to the Big Island — at least not to where we needed to go and return. While we waited for fuel, our crew would always walk to the restaurant and have pie for lunch. The vanilla ice cream melting over the hot crust and those apples covered with sugar and cinnamon was something impossible to forget. Maui is an ok island, but it's not my favorite. It's not nearly as beautiful as some of the lesser known or visited islands. Barbara insisted that we make the drive up the road to the Haleakala volcano when we visited Maui. The view at sunrise was supposed to be spectacular. We left our hotel room very early in the morning to make the drive. Unfortunately, we left a little too late and missed sunrise by about twenty minutes. People were making the drive down as we were driving up. It was another fail on my part. Pilots are supposed to know this kind of stuff. At least that's what Barbara thought. Hey, I was a helicopter pilot not an astronaut.

We had to be careful as we flew south from Maui to the big island. The terrain in Maui is mountainous all around. The wind picks up speed as it gets vectored through the valleys. It creates downdrafts and turbulence. The inexperienced pilot can be in for a shock. It's not unusual to find yourself descending at several thousand feet per minute while attempting to climb. That's why no one flew the islands without having an experienced pilot show them the ropes. Even the most experienced pilots were taken aback on their first trip.

It was another seventy-nine miles from Maui to the Big Island. They call it the Big Island because it contains more than half of all Hawaii's land mass. It's the largest island in the United States. However, it only has thirteen percent of Hawaii's population. It's an ideal place for Marine and Army forces to conduct live-fire training. We flew to the Pohakuloa Training Area. Pohakaloa means high rocky cinder cone in the Hawaiian language. PTA is located in the high plateau between the Mauna Loa, Mauna Kea, and the Hualalai volcanic mountains. We flew into Bradshaw Army Airfield's single military airstrip there. Flying around Maui was dangerous but flying into Bradshaw was treacherous. As we flew up the mountain, we overflew Parker Ranch where Hawaiian cattle roamed freely. The volcanic terrain slopes gradually from the shore to more than six-thousand, eight-hundred feet. The slope is so gradual that one barely notices. Many a pilot has been deceived by this optical illusion. When the temperature is warm, density altitude becomes a factor. For non-pilot types, density altitude is pilot talk for thinning air. As temperature and altitude increase, air thins and can hamper an aircraft's ability to climb or keep flying when heavy. As we made the climb up to PTA, we noticed the many puus — steep hills created by volcanic action — scattered among the sparse vegetation. Once at the top, I witnessed one of the strangest things I have seen as an aviator. The windsocks at either end of Bradshaw Airfield's runway were pointing at each other. The wind was whipping around both sides of the Mauna Loa volcano. No matter which way we landed, we would be landing downwind. It was safer to perform a running landing than to attempt to hover with the wind to our backs at that altitude.

We flew to PTA whenever Marines were training there. Normally, CH-46 helicopters made the trip. However, every so often, we shared the load and stayed there overnight in one of the steel buildings left there from WWII training days. There wasn't much to do at PTA for the helicopter crews except to tend to our aircraft. There was always something to work on. We pilots didn't help much. We wouldn't know what to do. Maintaining helicopters took specialists. Their work was never complete. Pilots could walk around or sit and play cards. Walking in volcanic terrain gets old really quick. It helped to bring a good book. After a few nights at PTA, we made the return trip to Oahu.

Sometimes, we had to fly into General Lyman Field in Hilo. Hilo is on the southern shore of the Big Island. That was always an interesting trip because Hilo had the best flowers in Hawaii. I always bought an exotic arrangement with Bird of Paradise, pink anthuriums, Hawaiian Kona Coffee flowers, and Proteus and Ginger. It never hurt to have a few brownie points racked up with the wife. On the way back, we would fly past the active Kilauea volcano and watch the red-hot lava flow to the ocean. The black sandy beaches of Punalu'u and Polakolea were always two of our favorite attractions. If we were lucky, we might sight sea turtles swimming in the surf. As we got closer to Lanai we looked for whales. Sometimes if we were lucky, we might catch a glimpse of humpbacks as they breached. We didn't bother them though. That could get us in big trouble with the conservationists.

Another favorite trip was to fly Northwest from Oahu to Kauai. That flight was a little over one hundred and eight miles. Kauai was another beautiful island with many mountains and valleys. One of our favorite spots to visit there was the fern grotto. It was located on a narrow river and only accessible by boat. It featured caves where long ferns and exotic flowers hung down and framed their entrances. Often, couples held their weddings there. The acoustics were perfect for Hawaiian singers strumming their ukuleles.

I was stationed in Hawaii from July of 1980 through July of 1984. While there, I deployed twice. I spent six months onboard the USS New Orleans and six months onboard the USS Belleau Wood. Both were helicopter carriers. The ships sailed all over the western Pacific. Barbara and my daughters stayed in Oahu. Unlike a lot of families, they never got island fever — an uncontrollable itch to get off the island and back to the mainland. After I spent four years in the Washington, DC area, flying for the White House and attending the Marine Corps Command and Staff College, they sent us back to Hawaii for another three years. Neat, huh? We loved Hawaii. We had plans to retire there at one point. However, before we went back, Japanese investors bought up a great deal of real estate on Oahu. The prices skyrocketed. We couldn't afford a shack there on military pay. So, we waited until our next duty station in Southern California before we bought a home. Although we settled in California, our hearts still long for Hawaii.

CHAPTER 26

Crossing the Line

We left Phuket, Thailand more than a week before. As the ship rocked and pitched gently over the waves, Rooster, Button, Clark and I listened to Ernest Tubb's rendition of an old sailors' song, Filipino Baby, on my tape recorder. As Ernest crowed about the warships leaving Manila, there was pounding on our stateroom door. I knew it was time. Rooster and my other two roommates rolled over in their racks to face me. I knew they enjoyed being on the other end of this. I could see the glee in their eyes as they were grinning ear-to-ear. Grinning, because they had nothing to worry about. They had already gone through the "initiation." They were already "Trusty Shellbacks." I jumped out of the rack and pulled on my trousers. I knew it was inevitable. "Don't forget the knee pads and gloves," Button reminded me. "You're going to need 'em, Libbo." As I donned the gloves and pulled the knee pads over my utility trousers, the pounding at the door got louder and more urgent. They were relentless. It was payback time. It was 6 AM on Wednesday morning, April 20th, 1983. My enlisted flight crew had come calling. It was time to face my "crimes."

We had been at sea for several months, sailing from Hawaii aboard the USS New Orleans (LPH-11) — a helicopter aircraft carrier. We already made port calls to Guam, the Philippines, Korea, Hong Kong, Singapore, and Thailand. We flew in military exercises throughout the Pacific Ocean. Now the ship was in the Indian Ocean and headed to Freemantle — a port on the western shore of Australia. Once there, Marines from HMM-265 would participate in "Valiant Usher." Valiant Usher was a joint military exercise with the Australian Marines and Navy, which took place on the western shores of Australia. During Valiant Usher, Marines from both countries would assault an imaginary enemy on the beach and the "outback" north of Perth. The long trek from

Thailand required us to sail through the Malacca Strait to the northern tip of Sumatra. There, the ship turned south and sailed through the South China Sea toward the Indian Ocean. During the night, we had "crossed the line" — sailed over the equator — and it was game on!

When a ship "crosses the line," the Navy holds a "line-crossing ceremony." It's a tradition that dates back more than four-hundred years. It hails back to the days of yore — the days of "Wooden ships and Iron Men." The ceremony calls for those who have never crossed — "Slimy Pollywogs" — to be initiated into the "mysteries of the deep" by those who have crossed — "Trusty Shellbacks." During the ceremony, Pollywogs are required to undergo humiliating and protracted torment — all in "good fun." All "Hands" voluntarily go through the ceremony, regardless of their military rank or standing. It's possible to "opt out," but few do. It's an ancient test of character for all.

After I was read my "crimes" — all "scurrilous lies" — by my flight crew. I was forced to join the other "Slimy Wogs" on the flight deck. There, they tied a collar around my neck and put me in line with the other "Wog Dogs." Whack! Whack! Whack! The Shellbacks were swatting the backsides of the "Wogs," who slowed their "Wog-Dog" parade with short lengths of fire hoses. Whack! Whack! Whack! I kept my forehead pressed against the rear of the Wog in front of me — any openings between Wogs would be mercilessly exploited with a swat. We had to keep things moving — keep crawling forward — so we could all "enjoy" being pelted with rotten fruit and garbage. Suddenly, about half way down the deck, the line of Wogs stopped. We reached King Neptune, Davy Jones, her Highness "Amphiitrite," and their "Court" of characters dressed in drag. It was time to kiss the "Royal Baby's Belly" coated with axle grease and hair. I nearly lost Tuesday night's dinner while getting my face squished and rubbed into the fat baby's belly. I rejoined the Wog parade. It was time to crawl through a canvas chute filled with rotting garbage and hair cropping from the barbershop. Half way through the chute, the line of Wogs ahead of me stopped. Some Shellback had halted the line to make sure that I got the full treatment. I tried to keep from breathing in that foul smell, as I kneeled in that garbage, hair and vomit. It was useless. Out it came! I barfed-up Tuesday's dinner.

Crawling out of the chute, I looked up and saw the grinning faces of my flight crew. They were really enjoying themselves. "Get back in line, Wog!" one of them said. I rejoined the line of Wogs. We Wogs crawled forward with the garbage, hair and vomit on us from head to toe. Once I reached that basin filled with garbage and water, I climbed up on the edge. My flight crew threw me backward into the slimy water. I was "baptized." When I emerged from that basin of slimy water, I was greeted by my aircrew. I was now one of them. The bond had been forged. I was a "Trusty Shellback," and — in their eyes — a good sport, someone worthy of respect.

CHAPTER 27

The Ranch

It still seems like yesterday. We were at altitude in the Santa Ynez Mountains just north west of Santa Barbara. We were all standing around our hangar near the shining VH-3D. Some Marines still had rags in their hands from wiping down and polishing the aircraft. That was a ritual after each and every flight, no matter how long the flight lasted. He arrived driving an old jeep like the kind you see in World War II movies with several scruffy old farm dogs following. He looked relaxed in his flannel shirt, jeans, and cowboy boots. He wasn't wearing a hat, probably because another helicopter was set to arrive at any minute with his wife.

While he waited, he walked into the portable hangar. Although I had flown him there as a copilot, I didn't know whether to come to the position of attention or not. It didn't matter though, he had that casual way about him that put people at ease immediately. We could tell he was enjoying seeing us as he walked closer. I was still in awe. This was my first actual meeting, and I had never had a conversation with him. Before long, he was telling jokes, and the circle of Marines began to tighten around him. I can't remember the stories he told — I'm sure they were all good clean ones. We all laughed and looked at each other, basking in our good fortune that day. We had the best job on earth!

It was December of 1985, and we would spend a lot of time away from our families over Christmas. We got into this unit because we were all volunteers. That may seem silly to a lot of people; but given the length of time it required away from home, not everyone wanted the job. Of course, we had to pass an extensive background check and be proficient at what we did; but mostly it was because we volunteered and our peers had confidence in our ability.

Now, the usual military rules and protocol didn't always apply in this unit, particularly when it came to flying and being in Command of a detachment. For example, there was Steve Taylor — a Captain at the time — Steve was in Command of detachments that included pilots senior to him in rank. He might have two or three majors on a detachment that could go anywhere in the world. We had military orders that allowed us to go anywhere, at any time, by any means. We never knew where or when we might be leaving. That was a lot of responsibility for a company grade officer. Eventually, Steve would command that unit as a full colonel, flying various presidents all over the world as their personal pilot. I was happy to be there and make Presidential Aircraft Commander.

So, I was still getting used to all of this new stuff when President Ronald Reagan walked into the hangar and started cracking jokes to his Marines. When Nancy landed on the ranch's helicopter pad at the western White House, President Reagan bid us all farewell and walked out to meet her. As they drove off down the dirt road to the ranch house in that old jeep followed by those scruffy dogs, I thought, "Man what a life!"

CHAPTER 28

Capitol Steps

It wasn't the most direct route from Andrews Air Force Base. We deviated, as he requested, just enough to enhance the visual. We passed all the Washington historic monuments, allowing the press and television cameras to capture the moment for history. The spotlights by the Capitol steps were bright. The flashes from the cameras flickered like fireflies. It required concentration to set the helicopter gently on the ground. It wasn't just one landing, but three — tail wheel first, left main, then right. It took practice to keep that tail wheel from bouncing. Everything had to be done in slow motion. The pilots' actions had to be slow as molasses and precise. The aircraft had to settle on the long struts before the landing was complete. The rotor blades had to stop at just the right time and place. The crew chief then opened the door, exited, walked down the steps and aft, opened the rear door, and assumed his position by the front door before the President exited. It was all procedure — all a performance. It's the same every time. The pilot in the right seat gets the pressure. The pilot in the left seat gets the photo op. I remembered to turn my head. I was lucky. I was in the photo. This one was classic.

The ribbing began as soon as I entered the ready room. The other pilots made jokes about the shine on my shoes, about the length of my hair, and about my uniform. They could practically read my security badge. I hung it on the airframe over the left chin bubble. I had no idea what they were joking about. Then, one of them tossed me the morning issue of the Washington Post. There I was on page fourteen. The picture took up nearly half the page. It was me in black and white staring at the President as he exited Marine One on the Capitol steps. Major Monigan and I flew President Reagan from Andrews Air Force Base to the Capitol the evening before. President Reagan had just returned from the summit in Geneva. It was a historic moment. A moment captured for eternity by newspaper photographers and television crews. There was a video of the entire trip playing repeatedly on the television. We flew past the Washington monument in slow motion. It was just another routine lift. However, unlike other lifts, I was in the picture, and it made the paper. It wasn't just any paper. It was the Washington Post. I was frozen in black and white with the Reagan's for eternity. Well, you know what I mean.

It took a year of training just to get in the left seat. That's after 4 years of college and 9 years of Marine Corps training. It required two-thousand, five-hundred flight hours before I signed for the aircraft and moved to the right seat. Once in the right seat, the photo ops were gone — at least for me. Others like Steve Taylor and Dick Peasley spent multiple tours there for a total of eight years. That's a lot of time gone from your family. Eight years of being on the road. Eight years of being separated from your wife and kids. Eight years of living out of a suitcase in hotel rooms over the holidays. That's a big price to pay for a few photos. The funny thing is that the pay was just the same as if Steve and Dick had stayed closer to home. You have to ask yourself if it was worth it. You can't make up for the time away from your wife and kids. That time is gone forever. Yes, there will be photos on the wall with the President. What won't be on the wall are pictures of you and your family.

CHAPTER 29

More HMX-1 Memories

I've done some weird things in my life — things I never dreamt of doing. I've ridden in the back of Huey helicopters over the jungles of Vietnam. My legs have dangled out open aircraft doors as we skimmed triple-canopy tree tops. I've slept in the rain in muddy foxholes — ten thousand miles from my home with insects gnawing at my face. I've watched artillery and mortar shells explode above and around me. I've recovered from shrapnel wounds in Army field hospitals. I've landed helicopters on Navy aircraft carriers at night in the pitch blackness of the Atlantic and Pacific oceans. I've flown in formations of helicopters filled with Marines to the shores of countries throughout the Mediterranean, the Pacific, and places I never thought I would see. I've flown coast to coast across the United States in numerous types of helicopters. I've slept on remote balmy islands with giant coconut crabs clinging to the palm trees. I've attended the memorial services and funerals of my shipmates.

But, some days while assigned to HMX-1 were surreal. As an example — there we were — Dick Peasley and I in the cockpit of Marine One. We were on final approach to the helicopter pad at Vatican City. In the back of the VH-3D helicopter — sitting in his high back chair — was the President of the United States. It was the 6th of June 1987. Ronald Reagan was en route to an audience with Pope John Paul II. We landed there and later took President Reagan to see the Italian President at his residence. Thirty years later, I went back to Rome and the Vatican as a civilian. As I walked through Vatican City, I tried to remember the day we landed there. It just didn't seem real. It felt as though everything had been a dream.

Flying the President wasn't the only thing we did at HMX-1. Back when I was in the squadron, Pilots had many additional duties. I was an "Operational Test Director." As an OTD, I flew many operational test flights on the latest equipment that was fielded for Marine Corps helicopters. I also worked on many different "projects."

In 1987, I was sent with several other pilots to Israel to fly with the Israeli Air Force in order to evaluate their Night Vision Goggle Heads-up displays. While flying with several of their H-53D aircraft at night, our aircraft got a transmission chip light. We landed in a clear area followed by our escorts. As we waited for our mechanics to check the helicopter's transmission for chips, all of the pilots gathered in a circle near the aircraft. Brigadier General Iftach Spector was our Israeli sponsor and an Elbit Systems LTD executive. General Spector explained to the US pilots that it was the Israeli custom for each pilot to tell a war story while they waited for their aircraft to be fixed. So, the Israeli pilots began telling their stories. All of them flew jets as well as helicopters. It soon became apparent that I was outclassed in the aviation war story department. Unlike my friends, Stephen Pavlak, Bill VanNoy, Mike Williams, Robert Curtis and others who were highly decorated pilots from the Vietnam era, I had never flown in combat.

As they went around the circle, the Israelis told stories of their dog fights and their victories. Several were ACE's. I began to work up a sweat as my turn got closer. As the last pilot came close to finishing his story, I thought the best way out would be with humor. So, I congratulated them all for being great dog fighters, but told them that I was the only real "dog pilot," because I was the only one who flew the President's dog on Marine One. There was a lot of laughter that night, and I saved myself from a lot of embarrassment!

Being assigned to the Presidential Helicopter Squadron was a great experience. It was a hell of a lot of work, and I got to travel to places and fly various types of helicopters that I never would, otherwise. However, I was gone most of the time while assigned there — on the road and on the go for three years. It was tough on my marriage and the relationship with my girls. After three years,

I was ready to spend some time at home. When the opportunity to attend the Marine Corps Command and Staff College came, I jumped on it.

Looking back, I'm glad I served there — it was an honor. But I don't regret leaving when I did. Everything worked out for the best.

CHAPTER 30

Field Trip

It's the same nightmare every night. I jerk out of sleep. My head snaps forward. I rise out of bed like a monster in a Mel Brook's movie. It's always the same sequence — over and over. It's as if I'm an observer in years of the same bad dream. I'm always suspended in the air. I watch myself from above. People (men, women, Marines, soldiers and sailors) scream, gasp for breath. They choke. They moan and beg for help. They hang out the open windows.

To think I caused it has prevented me from sleeping for thirty years. I get out of bed. I splash cold water on my face. I try to shake it off. It never works. I'll never have a peaceful sleep again.

In the fall of 1987, I attend the Marine Corps Command and Staff College in Quantico, Virginia. It was a year-long school that covered many military subjects. There were a lot of lectures. There were a lot of guest speakers. There were also a few field trips. We went to Gettysburg. We walked the battleground. We walked in the field where General Pickett made his famous charge against the center of the Union's defense. We stood where Colonel Chamberlain and the 20th Maine held the Union left at Little Round Top. We went to Fredericksburg. We saw where Lee's army held against the Union as they crossed the Rappahannock River. We went to Georgia where we attended the Commander's Aviation Supply Course. We also went to Norfolk, Virginia. We boarded the Navy vessels berthed there. We went to Norfolk on a tour bus. The bus had air conditioning. It had a television with a VCR. We watched movies during the trip. The bus had food and drinks. The bus had a bathroom at the rear that was located above the bus's engine.

After touring the ships berthed in Norfolk, we were finished for the day. We decided to go out to dinner. Someone suggested a Mexican restaurant where the food was good. We went. We ate. We drank. We drank some more. We had a great time. The next day it was time to head back to Quantico. We loaded back on the bus. We watched a video on the TV. We talked and smiled. We were enjoying the ride. And, then it hit me. It was the Mexican food. My stomach was upset. My stomach was churning. I had to go. There was no holding it back. I left for the bathroom at the back of the bus. I closed the door. I did my business. It was hot back there. The fumes from the engine came up into the bathroom. I needed to get out of there. It was then that I heard it. I heard their screams. I thought there might be an accident. I thought there might be a terrorist attack. I pulled up my drawers. I zipped up and opened the door. People were hanging out the windows. People were screaming. People were pointing at me.

I haven't been able to forget. I haven't been able to get them out of my mind. Oh, the humanity!

CHAPTER 31

Clutch

No one in the history of the Marine Corps had done it — none that lived to tell the story. My Den Daddy was pissed! He had me locked at attention. He leaned in — his nose almost touching mine. His face was crimson. His eyes bulged. I thought they might pop out of his head. He would have screamed, if we hadn't been surrounded by so many foreign officers and dignitaries. "Clutch" McCutheon stood behind him. Clutch was laughing hard. I thought he might roll on the floor of the gymnasium. It was all Clutch's fault. He was a bad influence. I never did anything like that before I met Clutch.

Lieutenant Colonel Ray McCormick was our "Den Daddy." He was a member of the school's staff and responsible for supervising our conference group. Ray was infantry. He was a Vietnam Vet and was the commanding officer of a recon battalion. He chewed tobacco and had that typical grunt swagger. He was a good guy, though. Ray was at his terminal rank. Clutch and I may have put him there.

My conference group was an odd lot. Conference group seven had everything. We had naval aviators. We had grunts. We had everything from a communications officer to a female administrator. We had a Major from Jordan and a Lieutenant Colonel from the Philippines. Best of all, we had Gary "Clutch" McCutheon. Clutch was an F-4 Radar Intercept Officer. He had been assigned to Headquarters Marine Corps. He had been an infantry company commander. How he managed to pull that off is beyond me. Clutch had the personality of Harpo Marx. He never stopped clowning around. The instructors at the Command and Staff College gave up on trying to change Clutch. He was way beyond redemption. Eventually, they accepted his behavior. It was refreshing. His humor helped us get through the many boring lectures. I became Clutch's straight man. We had our own comedy team. It nearly got us in big trouble. It almost got Clutch killed.

Major Ahmed Abu-Al-Ghanam was an armor officer from Jordan. He had a lovely wife — Intisar. Clutch complimented her in front of Ahmed. It was a mistake. Ahmed took great offense. He told us that he would have to kill Clutch if they were in Jordan. I thought, "It's a good thing we aren't in Jordan, 'cause I really like Clutch." I wasn't so sure about Ahmed. He took offense at a lot of things — like the time Clutch put his feet on the table. The soles of his feet faced Ahmed. Ahmed was pissed. Apparently, that was a great insult. I thought, "There's no way Clutch is gonna make it through a year in the same room with Ahmed and come out alive." Ahmed's dress uniform included a Janbiya — a curved Arab dagger. I just hoped Clutch never stood next to Ahmed while we attended formal events. There was no telling what that crazy Jordanian might do to Clutch.

Clutch and I pulled a lot of shenanigans. There was the time we did a skit on stage in front of the whole class. Clutch put filling underneath my sweater to make it look like I had breasts. I stood at attention while Clutch pretended to be giving me an award. He wavered around. His hands went in circles. He pulled back each time he went to pin the medal on my chest. Finally, he gave up. He turned his head, closed his eyes and pinned it on my shoulder. We got big laughs. However, my solo attempt at humor was different. People just didn't do this in the Marine Corps.

It was a Halloween party dance at the Command and Staff College. We were supposed to go in costumes. The day of the party, I still hadn't thought of a costume. I ran out of ideas. The time to leave home got closer. Barbara and our daughters had an idea. Why not go as ballerinas? Both of my daughters took dance classes. We had their outfits. Barbara was an excellent seamstress. I thought, "Sure —why not — Clutch would do it." With a little modification, Barbara made ballerina outfits. We had the tutus, silk tights and tops. We fashioned some ballerina shoes with fabric over our sneakers. Barbara and the girls put on my makeup. I had a silk bow in my hair. I looked ridiculous. I didn't care. I wasn't worried about getting promoted. I was already a Major. I never thought I'd get that far.

When I walked in the gymnasium doors, the building went silent. Jaws dropped. Everyone stopped what they were doing. People stood and stared. The staff scurried for cover. Dignitaries in the bleachers leaned forward in their seats to get a better look. I took advantage. We stood on our toes. I twirled in circles as we entered to the sound of the music. I held my breath. Grunts ran the place. This could go sideways real fast. Their sense of humor wasn't the same as aviators. I must have confirmed their thoughts about Air Wingers. We were all nuts. We couldn't possibly be real Marines. That's when it happened. That's when Ray McCormick went ballistic and blew his top. He went in to his drill instructor act. The only thing keeping him from killing me were the many witnesses.

But, then things changed. It was the laughter. It was Clutch rolling on the floor. It was the entire gymnasium erupting in applause. Barbara and I danced. Everyone danced. We had a great time. I won the award for best costume.

CHAPTER 32

Gus

I don't remember the exact day. The newspaper article's date is missing, and the paper is faded. But, I bet Darren "Gus" Hargis remembers! After all, he was piloting the giant CH-53E helicopter when the nose wheel fell off in flight — strut and all — at Marine Corps Air Station Tustin, California. I think it was sometime toward the end of my tour with Marine Corps Heavy Helicopter Training Squadron, HMT-302; probably in the fall of 1993. For us Marines, it was just another exciting day at work. Well, maybe it was a little more exciting than usual for Gus, his crew, and me.

At the time, I was the Commanding Officer of HMT-302, a training squadron of some five-hundred Marines and sailors. Gus Hargis was one of approximately fifty pilots in the squadron — about half were instructors, and half students. Gus was a seasoned Iraq War combat veteran, who was filling time between deployments by instructing new pilots to fly the CH-53E. The CH-53E was the western world's largest and most powerful helicopter, and my squadron was charged with training all the new CH-53D and CH-53E pilots, mechanics, and aircrews for the Marine Corps.

I was probably in the ready room when we got the call. The ready room was where pilots hung out when they were waiting their turn to fly or just wanted to listen to the FM radio and find out what was going on with our flight ops. Since I was responsible for the outfit, I liked to keep an eye on what was happening in the air. If I recall it right, Gus and his student had just taken off when it happened. It must have been something to lift that huge aircraft into a hover only to see your nose mount and wheels tumble between your foot pedals underneath the chin bubble. I can still hear the surprise in Gus's voice when he called operations! There wasn't panic in his call; it was more like, "Oh Shit! Now what? Houston, we have a problem!"

Fortunately, for me this wasn't the first time I had seen something like this. I recall one of my friends having his right main mount blow up through the sponson on a CH-53D years earlier. Now that was a problem! The sponsons are on each side of the aircraft and house the landing gear main mounts and main fuel tanks. Once the main mount blew, he was missing the landing gear on the right side of the aircraft, had a damaged fuel system, and was flying off a Navy ship in the middle of the Atlantic Ocean! Lucky for him, cool heads prevailed, and Marines quickly brought mattresses up to the flight deck where they were strapped to the deck's tie down points and hosed down with water in time for him to make a safe landing. CH-53's create hurricane force-like winds. Hosing down the mattresses makes them heavier and less prone to blowing away while strapped down.

Once Gus made the radio call, curious bystanders started to gather around the radio in the ready room. Soon, they spilled out of the hangar to the parking lot in order to get a better look at the situation. Gus was hovering the helicopter above a cement helo pad where we taught new pilots the basics of taxiing and hovering. I got on the ready room FM radio and asked his status. He had a full load of fuel, and other than missing the nose gear, the aircraft and crew were OK. I ran out to the helo pad, and someone followed and gave me a portable FM radio. As the crowd began to gather, I instructed Gus to go burn off some fuel in order to lighten the aircraft — mattresses can only support so much weight. Gus took off and circled nearby the Air Station while the maintenance folks rounded up mattresses from the barracks and brought wooden pallets and straps from the warehouse.

While we waited for Gus to burn off fuel, the crowd began to grow. News spread quickly across the Air Station, and it wasn't long before we had a huge audience, including the Group and Station Commanders and their staffs. Cameramen from the Station Public Affairs Office also showed up, as well as reporters from the station paper looking for a story. It took about an hour and twenty minutes before we had the wet mattresses and pallets strapped in place and were satisfied that we were ready for Gus to make a landing. Once Gus dumped some fuel, I gave him the go ahead, and the big aircraft lumbered in to the helo pad.

As Gus maneuvered the helicopter over the mattresses and was about to set it down, a young enlisted maintenance Marine came running out of the hangar to the helo pad carrying an aircraft jack. Gus set the aircraft down above the mattresses perfectly while the young Marine guided the jack into position under the nose. Within a matter of minutes, the helicopter was on the ground. The crew shutdown the engines, and the rotor blades slowly spun to a stop. I breathed a huge sigh of relief, as Gus and his crew exited the aircraft unharmed with the helicopter otherwise intact.

To this day, I think of the difference one young Marine made. Just when I thought I had a problem solved, someone surprised me with a better idea! Putting that jack in place saved us a whole lot of work and made replacing the nose gear a simple job. It was always pilots like Gus and Marines who kept their cool that made us look good!

CHAPTER 33

Colors

I handed the shoebox to the retired general. I knew the gentleman. He wouldn't ask too many questions. "It's time for this to go home where it belongs," I said. "If anyone asks where I got it, just tell them I found it hidden away in a shoebox in an old building." He nodded his head and handed me some forms to fill out for the museum's files. We reminisced for a few minutes before I left the Miramar Air Station's aviation museum. I waved as I drove away.

Twenty-two years earlier, a platoon of Marines marched in tight formation on the Tustin Marine Corps Air Station flight line. Their M-16 rifles were perfectly aligned in a row over their right shoulders. The 3rd Marine Aircraft Wing Band led them and played the Marine Corps hymn. I held my salute as our nation's flag and squadron colors passed by. The platoon leader called, "Eyes right!" Marines snapped their heads right as their leader saluted. The parade was for me. Well, there were two of us standing there. But, I was the outgoing commanding officer. Lieutenant Colonel Jerry Yanello was the new CO. His parade would come later at the end of his eighteen-month tour. I stood and took one last long look at HMT-302's CH-53 helicopters on the flight line. It was sweet and sad at the same time. It was sweet because no one was hurt and no helicopters were damaged while I was in command. It was sad because it was my last official day as a Marine Corps officer. I decided to retire after a combined twenty-two years of service in the Army and Corps.

Being in command of Marines was the easiest job of my life. When I took over the squadron in 1992, I could see that the squadron's Marines needed to be given their head. They needed to be free to make decisions. A zero defects mentality had crept into the squadron and the Corps. People were afraid to make mistakes for fear of ruining their careers. Commanding officers felt they needed to micromanage everything their Marines were doing. They bombarded their Marines with questions and paperwork. They probed everything, leaving no stone unturned. Marines spent more time answering memos and questions than doing their jobs. I didn't like it. I didn't like it as an enlisted man in the Army. I didn't like it as a junior officer. I didn't like it when it came from my leaders. I didn't plan on passing that way of leading on to my Marines.

During our first all-officer's-meeting, I gave the officers my philosophy. I wasn't going to do their jobs for them. I didn't expect them to do their Marines' jobs. I could protect them as long as they stayed within the box. Once they got in trouble outside the box — meaning outside our squadron — there was little I could do for them. They were on their own. I also let them know that any Marine in the squadron could down an aircraft without exception. If someone felt an aircraft was unsafe to fly, it was down until our quality assurance professionals checked it over. I wanted my pilots to understand that there wasn't any training mission that was so important that it was worth damaging an aircraft or getting someone hurt. No one would question them if they felt it was unsafe to fly for any reason — whether it was the condition of the aircraft or weather. I let them know that I wouldn't tolerate anyone flat-hatting or flying dangerously. In ten years no one would remember what our aircraft availability was, how many flight hours we flew, or if we made our pilot training goals. However, if one person got hurt, they wouldn't forget it for the rest of their lives. I let them know that they weren't there to get me promoted. Their job was to pass as much knowledge as possible to the new pilots and aircrews we were training. We were at the end of our careers. Our students were just beginning theirs. We were the past. Our students were the future. I told them that I had two daughters — no sons. I wanted my daughters to have the same opportunities as we did. Sexual harassment would not be tolerated for any reason. Anyone who I caught disrespecting another Marine in that way would be run out of the Corps. I told them to pass it on to their Marines.

I tried to set the tone with maintenance the first day. The maintenance officer and his chief came to my office early Monday morning. They carried the aircraft status reports. Aircraft availability had been a problem, and we all knew it. Something was wrong. I had an idea what it was. The problem was coming from my office — not theirs. They had been told what to do and how to do it for too long. They wouldn't do anything unless they were ordered. So, I decided to test my theory. When they arrived in my office, I could see that they were defensive and loaded for bear. They expected me to grill them on every aircraft gripe. That's what happened in the past. They had charts and graphs to defend themselves. They planned on being in my office for hours arguing their case. They were wrong. I said, "Thanks, just leave the reports on my desk." They walked away stunned. I read the morning newspaper and put my feet up on my desk. I left the door open so people could see me as they passed by. I was sticking my neck out, but I had to give it a try.

Every squadron within the Aircraft Group had one training day per week. There wasn't any flying on those days except for functional test flights. Marines were expected to accomplish other training, such as required reading. Invariably, Marines ran out of things to do shortly after lunch. They sat idle for hours on training day afternoons. Our training day was Monday, which meant we flew on Friday. Marines had to work on Saturdays to fix any new problems that came up during Friday's flights. I decided to move our training day to Friday. That way, we could fly our test flights on Friday and leave our aircraft in an up status all weekend. Marines had an incentive to complete their work, so they could have the extra time off on Friday afternoon. They also had all weekend off since we didn't have to work on Saturday. They loved it. Once we changed our training day and I left them to do their jobs without meddling, aircraft availability immediately improved. By the time I retired, we had the highest availability in the Group.

It was the fastest eighteen months in my life and the most enjoyable. In my opinion, morale soared. People knew that they would have more time off, more time with their families, and less interference from me. When it was over, we had flown more than 5,000 hours and met all of our training goals while adding additional Marines to the squadron. When I left there were more than five-hundred Marines in HMT-302.

I was going through transition training prior to retirement. Those retiring or exiting the Marine Corps were required to attend classes that were supposed to help us make the transition to civilian life. Actually, they were quite depressing. We were told to expect less pay, less responsibility, and a tough time finding work. On my last day of class, I walked out the door and bumped into my squadron's Sergeant Major. He asked me if I was finished with classes. I told him I was and that I wouldn't be coming back. He handed me a soft, brown paper bag. He said, "Don't open this until you are off the base." It seemed like a funny thing to say, but I followed his instructions. When I got home, I opened the bag. Inside were the HMT-302 squadron colors — the squadron's flag.

The colors hung on a staff behind my desk for about ten years until Barbara decided to redecorate our home. All of my military things were put in boxes — all of my awards, wooden plaques, pictures, and memorabilia. The colors went in an old shoe box and sat in my closet for another twelve years. When I retired from my civilian job at the Marine Corps air station in Yuma, I cleaned out my closet and found the shoe box. I decided it was time for the colors to go back where they came from. There was a problem, however. The squadron had changed its name. My aircraft were obsolete. The squadron was flying tilt-rotors. The colors belonged in a museum where everyone could see them. So, one day I finally got around to taking them to the museum at the Miramar Marine Corps Air Station. When I handed them to the general, I was handing him my past. It was time to start over again. The HMT-302 colors are hanging proudly in the museum at the Marine Corps Air Station in Miramar, California.

CHAPTER 34

Jordan Yankov

Jordan was the straw that broke my back. After Jordan, I couldn't serve anymore. My heart wasn't in it. I was tired of the pain. I was tired of memorial services. I was tired of funerals. I couldn't face another grieving family.

When I met Jordan, we were stationed in Hawaii. I was an aircraft commander and the Marine Aircraft Group's CH-53D helicopter check pilot. Jordan was a feisty Chicago kid with a quick temper and a lot of desire. He was a few years junior to me and still a copilot. He was quick to learn and he had the necessary skills. He was what we called a "good stick." There was no doubt that he would pass his check rides. What he didn't have then was enough flight time. It required 500 hours to become an aircraft commander. Parts, funding, and flight time were scarce in 1980. Squadron pilots were flying five to ten hours each month at best. When Jordan approached four-hundred and ninety-five hours, Bob Leavitt and I played a trick on him. It was cruel. But, when Marines see someone's chain hanging out, they always pull it. All of the pilots in the squadron were in on the joke. We changed the requirements to be an aircraft commander from five-hundred to seven-hundred and fifty hours. You have to understand that being in command of an aircraft is a big deal to pilots. They have big egos that need to be stroked. It's their Achilles heel. Anyway, we had our administrative section draft a fake naval message — the official means of corresponding back then. We posted the message on the read and initial board outside the ready room. The message looked real. It had all the correct addressees and the official squadron stamp. It even had comments from the commanding officer giving instructions to the operations officer to take it for action. Once the trap was baited, we waited. It was just a matter of time before Jordan got around to reading it. When he did, his response was classic. There was a lot of bitching. He complained to everyone and anyone who listened. He was nearly in tears. We laughed our asses off.

Jordan and I became close friends. We deployed together in the Pacific. We spent six months at sea sailing everywhere. We played pong for hours on the computer in our stateroom. We wrestled like brothers. We went shopping in Singapore. We rolled pigs for drinks at the Bull and Bear pub in Hong Kong. We went bar hopping in the Philippines and Thailand. We rented a condo in Perth, Australia and roamed the town together. I watched him marry Margaret on the Flight Deck of the USS New Orleans. I saw Maggie transform him into a man. She rounded his rough edges. I held his children (Katherine and Nicholas) in my arms when they were born.

Jordan was heading home on a cross country flight when one of his rotor blades departed his aircraft due to intergranular corrosion. He and his crew were dead before they hit the ground. I tried to get out of going to Jordan's funeral. Maggie insisted that I attend. It would be unforgivable if I didn't. I knew it. I had to go. I'd never be able to live with myself. I dreaded facing her. She had two babies. What could I say? I'd say something stupid. I knew I would. I always did. No one trained me for this. Oh, they trained me. But, never for this. Winging it only made me sound stupid and crude. It was better to keep my mouth shut and just nod my head.

It was different this time. I bumped into her unexpectedly. She was with her escort in the elevator. I was trapped. She was dressed in black. I saw the tears behind her veil. I couldn't hold mine back. The escort officer was upset. This was not how I was supposed to act. I couldn't help it. Maggie knew it. She told him it was okay — that Jordan and I were close friends — that she and I were close friends. It was okay.

They gave Jordan military honors at the funeral. I stopped by the house. Maggie and I sat on the sofa. We tried to console Jordan's mother. I said some incredibly stupid things about how much he had contributed to the country. I could see she wasn't buying it. I should have kept my mouth shut.

Shortly after, I returned home. My twenty years was nearly up. As soon as it was, I submitted my retirement letter.

CHAPTER 35

Puppy

The base chapel was packed with Marines and civilians. Lieutenants were huddled together and crying near the stage. They were dressed in blues and stood close to the photograph of their friend. The photo was prominently displayed on a stand between stained glass windows. A row of lit candles flickered on either side. The Amature family were New Yorkers. They sat together silently in the front row. His mother was dressed in black and wore a veil. His father had his arm around her and held her as she leaned against his shoulder. I took an empty seat in the back near the exit. I learned that it was best to stay as far away as possible when I attended these events. If I got too close to the front or near the families, their pain might jump from them to me. I didn't want any more pain. I couldn't do my job if I allowed the pain. His squadron commander would talk to the family. I was relieved it wasn't me.

His demeanor was not what one expected of a Marine Corps officer. It was impossible not to like him. His call sign was perfect. They called him "Puppy." It was obvious once you met him. At twenty-seven, James Amature was so enthusiastic that he appeared to be wagging a tail. His grin was ear to ear. His eyes twinkled with delight. I forgot how it felt to be like him — enthusiastic, innocent, trusting, and confident in my seniors. I signed his copilot designation papers a few months before the mishap. After graduation, he went right into the action. His squadron went to Somalia and provided relief to starving civilians caught in a struggle for power. He flew in difficult conditions with little rest. When he returned to the states, he was all aglow — full of tales of his exploits — loving every minute of life. He came by my squadron. He wanted to see the instructors who had trained him to fly the CH-53D helicopter. He wanted to let us know that he was close to completing his aircraft commander checks. A few more flight hours, and he would sign for the aircraft. He was proud of his accomplishments. He should have been. He worked hard to get there.

I heard about it on the news. The reporter said that a Marine Officer was killed. Four others were injured. Their Tustin-based helicopter landed tail-first and burst into flames on the runway. They were landing at the Mountain Warfare Training Center in Bridgeport, California. I wondered who was killed. I wondered who the others were who were hurt. Every new pilot and crew member in the Marine Corps was trained by my squadron. I remembered most of them. I interviewed them before graduation. I tried to warn them about the dangers of the job they were undertaking. I tried to instill in them a sense of responsibility toward their passengers and fellow crew members. Still, these things continued to happen. On the afternoon of the 13th of March, 1994, Puppy was on a training flight. He was flying one of his last flights as a copilot. Flying in the mountains is tricky and dangerous. The winds are unpredictable. There are updrafts and downdrafts. There's turbulence. The aircraft doesn't respond as well at altitude. The air is thinner. It takes more power. It takes experience. The others involved in the mishap survived. I'm sure that their lives were never the same.

The Chaplain said a prayer. He read their names. The congregation sang songs. Puppy's friends eulogized him. They sang more songs. When it was over, I exited through the back door. I had students to train.

CHAPTER 36

Dianna

I couldn't believe it! After twelve years of civilian life, the Marine Corps wanted me back. Well, it wasn't exactly the Corps that wanted me. Science Applications International Corporation had a contract with the Marine Corps, and SAIC wanted me. After I retired from the Corps, I worked as a superintendent at one of the many terminals where ships loaded and unloaded on the docks of Long Beach, California. Longshoremen did the labor. Superintendents were responsible for supervision. I hated the job. Yet, I stuck it out for twelve years.

I was caught in a monkey-trap. After retiring from the Corps, I grabbed on to a banana — a decent salary with benefits. I wouldn't let go. It didn't matter how much I hated the job. I resigned myself to working under miserable conditions for the rest of my working life. For twelve years, I hated work. For twelve years, I was nauseous as I entered the terminal gate. I felt like I was in the movie, *Ground Hog Day*. Every day was the same. Nothing changed. Longshoremen were among the highest paid workers in the world with fabulous benefits. They had it made. They flipped coins to see who would go home. Nearly half the labor force was gone before the shift started. Yet, they were the most unhappy, discontented people I ever met. People pulled the same crap every day. Labor slowed down as much as possible. People refused to cooperate. People complained constantly. It was culture shock leaving the Marine Corps and walking into that bunch. I was used to people who were enthusiastic about their jobs. I was used to being part of a team. I was used to great leadership. None of that applied on the waterfront. Everyone was in it for themselves. Eventually, I was in it for myself.

Then it happened. I read an advertisement for a job with SAIC in Yuma, Arizona. The job required the applicant to be a former Naval Aviator and a graduate of the Marine Corps' elite tactics training squadron — Marine Aviation Weapons and Tactics Squadron One. I attended MAWTS-1 in 1982 as a student in one of their first classes. That was twenty-four years earlier — twenty-four years! It didn't matter that it was so long ago. A government contract requirement was a firm requirement. I answered the add by email on a Friday; SAIC called me Monday morning. It was surreal! An SAIC executive interviewed me by phone and hired me on the spot. I gave two weeks' notice, and I was free.

I told Barbara that I was thinking of taking the contractor job in Yuma. She took one look at me and knew that I had already accepted the job. She didn't resist. She was glad for me. She practically packed my bags. Barbara's sister lived in Yuma, so it wasn't all that bad. Barbara visited us on weekends, or I drove back to California. My weekends were free. It was a five day a week, eight hours a day job. I was used to working sixty hours a week at nights without knowing my next day off. This was heaven! To top it off, I got a raise and got to work with Marines again. It was the best decision and luckiest work-related break of my life. I was going home.

When I checked into MAWTS-1, it was apparent that I had a lot of catching up to do. Everything had changed. Things were computerized. The communications people had their own language. They talked in acronyms that I had never heard before. It was all about Link-16, IP addresses, connectivity, and protocols. It took fifty steps just to program one of their radios. The operations people were working with aviation platforms that didn't exist when I was on active duty. Now, they communicated with airborne platforms by data links. It was a rude awakening. Hell, we didn't have computers or email when I served. I wondered if I would ever be able to catch up.

One of the first people I met and worked with at MAWTS-1 was a female lieutenant. There weren't a lot of women in the Marine Corps when I was on active duty. Most women were in the administrative offices. Dianna DiToro Budrejko was quite a surprise. Pound for pound, she was one of the best athletes in the

Marine Corps. Her petite stature belied her strength. At thirty-two, she power-lifted heavy weights and ran marathons for fun. She was stronger and ran faster than most men. I'm sure she was stronger than me. Dianna preferred the male physical fitness test. The men's test allowed her to perform pull-ups. She embarrassed the most physically fit Marines because she could lift her weight repeatedly as well as any male. Her arms were firm but not too bulky or veiny. They were all lean muscle. There wasn't an ounce of fat on her lithe body. She was also extremely intelligent. Dianna was a Pennsylvanian and a graduate of Old Dominion. She held a Bachelors in Exercise Therapy and a Masters in Organizational Leadership. She was also a seasoned veteran. She completed a combat tour in Iraq while working as a Direct Air Support Control Officer. Dianna helped me get back up to speed. She provided critical information and input that I used in my reports. She was a veritable encyclopedia of aviation information. She helped carry me through my first year back working with the Corps.

Dianna was married. Her husband was a "Bull" of a Marine from Connecticut. He was a Major who was also assigned to MAWTS-1 as an instructor pilot. Bull was a seasoned officer. He was a third generation Naval Aviator and Naval Academy graduate. He wore his father's "Wings of Gold." He completed five combat tours - Kosovo, Afghanistan, and three tours in Iraq. The Marine Corps decorated him twenty-five times for valor. Thomas "Bull" Budrejko had the killer instinct. He went for the jugular. I suppose as an attack helicopter pilot, he needed to be like that. His aircraft community ate their own. With them, it was sink or swim. Only the best need apply. The weak were weeded out. Only the strong survived. After all, they provided close air support to infantry Marines. Their war was up close and personal. They routinely flew into the jaws of death and brought lethal ordinance to bear on the enemy. It was kill or be killed. Getting shot down meant losing your head — literally. More than once, Bull's helicopter was riddled with bullet holes when he limped back to safe territory.

Tom was an exceptional athlete and had a sharp mind. He was a wrestler in high school and college. He played football and ran track. He had a body builder's physique. He was also intelligent. He graduated from the Naval Academy with a degree in Aeronautical Engineering. He held a Masters in Military Science from the Marine Corps Command and Staff College. Tom was on the path to the wear the stars of a General Officer — provided he kept his nose clean. He was also a bully. That's why his call sign was "Bull." Tom was the "top dog" in his attack helicopter community. He was sarcastic and caustic. He enjoyed needling and belittling his peers and juniors. That's what Marine Corps attack helicopter pilots do. That's what makes them different from transport pilots — it's their killer instinct and desire to be the best — to always be on top — to always have the last word — to always win the fight — to always pin their opponent and make them submit. That kind of competitiveness works well for a Marine Corps attack pilot — not so much for a husband. Combine that with a touch of PTSD, and Tom was headed for trouble.

Dianna and Bull had a son shortly after leaving MAWTS-1 and moving to Camp Pendleton. Little Andrew was born with a heart defect. They nearly lost him. His heart was plumbed backwards. It took numerous operations before he was straightened out. His medical condition put a lot of stress on Bull and Dianna's relationship. There was also the competitiveness between them. They were both type A personalities. Bull was bigger and stronger. Women can't make up for the additional fifty pounds of muscle and testosterone. He was also senior in rank to Dianna. Bull expected submission just as in his wrestling experience. Dianna was not one to submit to any man. She had her own ambitions. Bull's cutting remarks and sarcasm may have worked well with his fellow pilots, but they began to wear on their relationship. Slowly but surely, they tore at the fabric of their marriage. Dianna was an attractive woman. Men still turned their heads when she passed by. She felt conflicted. She didn't need to settle for a hostile relationship. There were plenty of other men available if she wanted change.

When it happened, Bull and Dianna's marriage was on the rocks. They had separated. That's not to say that they no longer loved each other. The relationship between a man and a woman is complicated. Love is complicated. Love doesn't stop just because there are difficulties in a marriage. There are ups and downs in every relationship. This relationship was no different. Things may have worked out. But, we will never know. On the evening of the 22nd of February, 2012, things changed forever. All opportunities for reconciliation were lost. LtCol Thomas "Bull" Budrejko's helicopter collided with another helicopter during night maneuvers. The mishap killed him and 6 others. Why it happened will never be known. Someone was distracted. No one knows who or why. Was Bull's mind on something or someone else when he should have been concentrating on flying? Was Bull thinking of her? Does she share the blame? The unanswered questions burn a hole in Dianna's soul. Only God can answer those questions.

Dianna buried herself in homework and exercise after the accident. It was her way of overcoming her grief and guilt. She left active duty and joined the Marine reserves. She completed a Doctorate in Physical Therapy. She was still an attractive woman. Men were still interested. They pursued her. For a time, she thought she had found love again. But there was a lot to overcome. She had been married to a superstar. Not many men could fill those shoes. Not many men would feel comfortable with a woman as accomplished as Dianna. It would take someone like Bull to not be intimidated by that kind of woman.

Her life is still complicated. She found success in her career as a Marine reservist. She and Andrew have traveled the world together. But, little Andrew is still left without his father. Dianna was left with a son who wants answers. Andrew is too young to understand that his Daddy is gone forever. He is too young to accept Dianna's explanations — too young to forget the hero he loves.

CHAPTER 37

The Stranger

It must have been seven or eight years ago when my best friend, Stephen "Pav" Pavlak, and I were sharing a bottle of one of our favorite chardonnays at Yuma's best kept secret — The Old Town Wine Cellar. We liked going there for a lot of reasons. It was the coolest place in Yuma — temperature wise, and the old Sears Roebuck & Company building provided a unique setting for enjoying a drink and conversation. We both enjoyed the wine and craft beer selections that were handpicked by the owner — Michael Shelhammer. But more than anything, it was the diverse group of interesting locals who frequented the place that kept us coming back. Most, but not all, were baby-boomers. Some were teachers, lawyers, doctors, nurses, store or restaurant owners, or military folk or contractors who worked at either Yuma Proving Grounds or the Marine Corps Air Station. We all had one thing in common — we liked having a beverage and conversation in a quiet place with friends. That, and of course, there were some unspoken rules that we lived by there.

Michael Shelhammer has a simple business model. He offers a variety of wine and craft beer selections that represent the best value for your money. He personally samples every beverage at home before a bottle has the honor of finding a place in one of his racks. He also maintains the old-fashioned etiquette that younger generations no longer seem to cherish. When it's crowded there and women enter the cellar, men quickly vacate their seats at the bar until the women either decide to take a seat, stand, or sit elsewhere. I remember one younger woman telling me that I didn't't need to get up when she walked in. I gave a slight nudge with my elbow toward Mike and told her, "Yes, I do. I'd like to be able to come back." Mike doesn't tolerate impolite people or drama; and he doesn't cater to those who talk loudly or cause a ruckus. It's a nice, peaceful, old place run by a well-mannered, old-fashioned guy. If you look close enough, you'll see photographs of beloved customers who have passed on — locals who are no longer with us — discretely hanging on the walls.

Now, Pav can be a little eccentric. Once you get to know him, you understand why. You see, Pav had been a young Army helicopter pilot in Vietnam almost fifty years ago. Pav had been shot down more times in his helicopters than I had been shot down trying to pick up girls as a teenager — and that was a lot! He's the only person who I know who has been shot at and hit on both ends — head and butt! So, when I said he was eccentric, what I really meant was that he could be a little sensitive to some things. You gotta understand, for some unknown reason, some men want to be a member of a club that Pav sometimes wishes he didn't belong to — the Vietnam War Survivor's Club.

So, that's why Pav's head lifted and turned toward me when a stranger our age joined our conversation at the bar. He had dropped a few words that indicated that he too had been an Army Vietnam helicopter pilot. The stranger had walked into the cellar about a half hour earlier and was enjoying a bottle of Laetitia Reserve Domaine pinot noir with his "trophy wife." I could see the unmistakable questioning on Pav's face as he tightened his jaw and squinted at this guy with a look that silently cried, "Bullshit!" The odds of three Vietnam veterans being in the same bar, at the same time — two of them Army helicopter pilots — in that tiny desert town were astronomical! Someone was an impostor. He had heard it all before. It usually went something like, "I was a Navy Seal," or "I was with Special Forces," or "I was a sniper," and of course, their military records were always "classified." For some reason, the same guys who didn't want to be in the service during that era were now pretending to be card carrying Vietnam combat vets. Pav usually wouldn't listen to any of it. He had heard it too many times before. They all eventually folded under his questioning. But, this time, rather than call him out, Pav kept his cool and let it slide — the stranger wasn't bragging. I was proud of him. Life is too short to let this stuff bother you. The war is over.

Pav even invited this stranger and his wife over to dinner at his home — "Pavstead." I was amazed!

I still remember that evening when Bill VanNoy and his lovely wife, Darla, walked into the dining area at Pavstead. I wasn't ready for it though! Bill was carrying a folder under his arm and a bottle of his favorite pinot. He put the bottle on the island that separated the kitchen from the living room and laid the open folder down on one of the stools. "There," he said. "I know you didn't believe me when we were at the wine cellar; so, let's just get this out of the way, so we can enjoy the rest of the evening." Pav and I exchanged our secret looks. Reluctantly, Pav picked up a fading parchment paper from the folder. He looked at it for a moment; and then, stone-faced, he handed it to me. As I looked at that nearly fifty-year-old document, I felt a flush of embarrassment flow from my neck to my forehead. I must have been bright red. Holy Shit! It was a Distinguished Flying Cross!

Now, you could probably fake a Distinguished Flying Cross if you were really sick and demented, but there was no doubt that this was real. It had Bill VanNoy's name on it, plain as day! He had been a CH-47 pilot. I've only seen that award a few times. My friend Robert Curtis — also a former CH-47 pilot — has one; and a few retired Generals I know have them. For military people, it's awarded for heroism in flight. For civilians, it can be awarded for extraordinary achievement in flight. Notable recipients include Amelia Earhart, Charles Lindberg, Robert E. Byrd, and George H. Bush. So, when I looked at that paper, I was completely embarrassed. It was like asking Charles Lindberg to see his pilot's license!

Well, time has moved on. I've gotten over my embarrassment, and Pav and I have gotten to know Bill and Darla. Bill got out of the Army and became an Aeronautical Engineer and Chief Pilot for Boeing. Darla was also a manager for Boeing. They both had extraordinary careers. Now, they run a touring company with two of their friends, Bill and Sandy Evans — VanEvans Tours, LLC. Pav and I have even joined them on several of their company's tours to Italy.

Now, I'm sure that when the next stranger enters the Old Town Wine Cellar and talks of a Vietnam experience, Pav will be giving that secret, squinty look to his friends at the bar — Bill and Darla VanNoy.

CHAPTER 38

Tank

I knew it. I could see it. I could tell.

He was drinking too often. He was drinking too much. He wouldn't stop. Others went home. He stayed. The bartenders knew it. He fell off the stool. They cut him off. He went somewhere else. He drove there drunk. He weaved. He missed the light. They stopped him. He went to jail. It didn't matter. He went back. He kept drinking. His life was at the bar. His friends were there. They played games. They watched sports. They held parties. It was always at the bar.

He was once a sports star. He was once a hero. He once had a family. He once had a good career. He never looked forward. He only looked back. He couldn't see the future. He could only see the past.

His life was a mess. His money went to booze. He bought his friends drinks. He stayed out all night. He lost his license. He lost his job. He lost his family. He lost his sober friends. He lost hope. He lost his will to live.

It was late. I was in bed. The phone rang. It was him. He was home. He was sick. He needed a ride. Could I help? I said, "sure." I got dressed and went over. I had a key. I went in. He was hugging the commode. It was full of blood. I called 911. The ambulance came. They took him away.

I went to the hospital. He was in bed wearing a hospital gown with an IV hanging off his arm. He looked bad. He was pale. He looked tired. We talked. I told him he needed to stop. He was killing himself. He agreed. He recovered. He went home.

I drove him to the doctor's office. I waited outside. The doctor told him to stop. I begged him to stop.

He tried. It didn't last. He missed the bar. He missed his bar friends. He missed the bar games. He missed the bar parties. He missed drinking. He liked the taste. He liked the buzz. He could talk there. He could open up there. They knew him there. He was somebody there. They respected him there. They drank with him. They got drunk with him. They picked him up off the floor. They called the cabs. They gave him rides. They took him home.

I was in California. It was late. I got the call. It wasn't him. It was his friend. He was in the hospital. "Just letting you know." I got out of bed. I got dressed. I packed my bag and I drove four hours.

I got to the hospital. I went to ICU. He was in bed. He had tubes and he was on a respirator. There were a few friends with him. He wasn't conscious. He didn't have much time. I asked to be alone. I talked to him. I told him I cared. I told him I loved him. I told him that I would miss him. I said goodbye.

CHAPTER 39

Motorcycles

There's something therapeutic about riding a motorcycle. I know it's dangerous. Maybe that's why it's healing. When I ride, I'm doing something that I enjoy. But, I know it can kill me. It's similar to flying helicopters. It takes all of your concentration to stay alive. You must keep your mind on the road. You have to be aware of your surroundings. You have to be able to predict the behavior of the of people in the cages around you.

The love for riding is something only motorcyclists understand. I think it's addictive. Motorcycles should come with a warning about the hazards of addiction. It's about the turning of the wheels and the open air. It's about the wind in your face and chest. It's about the exhaust note — how it changes with each shift of the gears. It's about the changing scenery — the twisty roads — the acceleration in turns and deceleration after. To really enjoy it, you can't care about where you are going. You shouldn't worry about when you have to be back. The true enjoyment comes from not knowing where you are headed. You will know it when you get there. It's kind of like the decisions in my life. I never planned a thing. Things just happened. I came to a fork in the road and took one. I didn't think twice about whether I was on the right road. I just kept going until the next fork.

I've ridden motorcycles since I was a kid. My first motorcycle was a Honda 50. I got it during my freshman year in high school. I didn't have a driver's license — so, I was confined to riding it on and around Willard Beach. You could do that back in the sixties. No one complained about Phil Upton and me zooming on the waterfront's mud at low tide in the evenings. Seriously, what could we hurt except ourselves — a few clams? We rode at the edge of the water from the "Point" to Fort Preble and back. We even rode in the winter — the ice and snow didn't stop us.

The Honda was a good bike for learning the basics of shifting, braking, and for understanding the mystery of turning. Turning a motorcycle is exactly the opposite of what you might think. It has something to do with "gyroscopic effects." It's called counter-steering. Without getting into the physics of it, let's just say that it messes people up when they first start riding. Braking is different too. Most of the braking power is in the front brake — about seventy-five percent. Riding a motorcycle requires coordination. It requires using both hands and feet to operate the controls — like controlling a helicopter. Like flying, your head has to be on a swivel. Trust me — danger is all around.

My next motorcycle was a Yamaha 250 cc Big Bear Scrambler. It was a much bigger bike. The engine was much larger and it was a two-cycle. Two-cycles really wind up fast. However, they weren't very reliable back in the sixties. The engine would foul because of an incorrect fuel - oil mixture. That bike was scary fast up to about eighty mph — then it topped out. Paul Pennisi did a wheelie and wrapped my bike around a telephone pole on Willow Street at Willard Beach. He underestimated its acceleration. It put him in the hospital. He was lucky he didn't kill himself. I was lucky we didn't get sued.

I've had a lot of bikes over the years — Hondas — Harley's — Suzuki's and BMWs. Lately, I've stuck with BMWs. I like the German engineering. The BMW engine is more like an aircraft engine — it hums. That's how BMW started — by building aircraft engines. When Germany was banned from building aircraft after World War I by the treaty of Versailles, BMW switched to building motorcycles. BMW has a cult following like Harley-Davidson does. BMW riders are completely different than Harley riders, though. Harley riders are into chrome and their bike's exhaust note. That's OK. I like Harleys too, now that I've ridden John Kimball's bikes. John's Road King is a very comfortable bike that floats over the road like one of those big Cadillacs from back in the 50's. BMW riders are into gadgets. When you go to a BMW rally, you see a lot of gadgets. They hang everything that you can imagine on their bikes — altimeters — barometers — radar detectors — CB's — long range fuel tanks — deer whistles. You name it — they have it. The Harley rallies are more fun, provided you don't get caught up in gang violence. They like to party and have a wild time. The BMW guys like to sit by their camp fires and discuss their latest gadgets.

Once I retired from flying helicopters, I started going on long motorcycle trips. Riding motorcycles was as close as I could get to recreating the feeling of flying. Flying and riding motorcycles are both dangerous. It doesn't take much to get in trouble. So, I don't recommend riding unless you are already hooked. If you are already hooked, find a bike that fits your body and riding style. A lot of guys I know will only ride Harley's. They like the sound and feel. Mostly, I think they like the lower seat position. They like being able to put both feet on the ground at a stop. Most people can't do that on a BMW. For some reason their bikes are tall. I think because the people from Bavaria are tall. European's make their seat position several inches taller than on American bikes. It takes some getting used to. If you are going to ride in a hilly place like San Francisco, you are much better off on a Harley. Stopping while going up those steep hills can get really scary on a BMW. I know. It scared the hell out of me when I stopped half-way uphill at a stoplight. Holding that bike up and keeping it from rolling back with only one foot on the ground took every ounce of strength I had. I thought I was going to die. Next time, I'll go around the city instead of cutting across the center.

I've ridden my bikes all over the place. I've ridden from California to Maine and back — to Alaska and back — Florida and back — and to many other places. Now, much of the fun in riding depends on who you are riding with — if anyone. Most of my trips have been solo — except for the trip to Alaska and a few trips around southern Maine with my Maine buds. I don't mind riding alone. If I'm riding alone, I have no one to blame but myself for not having a good time. I've been on some trips I didn't enjoy so much because of the people I was riding with — well, it was more their riding style that I didn't enjoy.

I really enjoy riding with my friends from Maine. Those guys are fun. They also have unique riding styles that make their trips more interesting and enjoyable. When you ride with these guys, it's best to understand them. Take Rick Hansen for example. His trips usually start with an airplane ride across country to somewhere like Phoenix, San Francisco, or Salt Lake City. Rick likes to ride Harley Road Kings. He really loves that bike. He owns one in Maine. Rick attempts to rent that bike whenever he goes on one of those long trips. If you are going on a motorcycle trip, it's always nice to have Rick around. Besides being a nice guy, he's very detail oriented. He always plans the trips well in advance. I think it has something to do with his professional work as a project manager. He puts together spreadsheets that detail everything about the trip. He has all the way-points mapped out. He marks the distances between way-points — the rest stops — the fuel stops — the restaurants — and the things to see at each stop. He makes the hotel reservations in advance. He even pays for the rooms in advance and decides who is rooming together each night. He sends us a bill at the end of the trip with a complete breakdown of the costs. Yes, it's good to have Rick along. Oh, Rick also likes to ride fast — not crotch-rocket fast — but fast. One thing, though. Don't touch Rick's bike. I'm just warning you. It doesn't matter if it's a rental. Only Rick touches Rick's bike.

Stan Davis also likes to ride fast. He also likes the Road King when he's on a trip without his cruiser. We usually let Stan and Rick ride together. I don't know if they are racing each other or not, but they tend to disappear after a few miles. That's ok. With Rick's spreadsheet, we know exactly where to find them if they get too far ahead. Usually, we will pass them as they pull over to take videos of us riding by. I've noticed that they do that a lot. Now, lately I'm concerned about Stan. He's starting to ride like an old man — he leaves his turn-signal on. The last few times I've ridden with him, he's ridden for miles with his turn-signal blinking. That worries me. Stan says just to honk if we see that he's left his signal on. But, if he's miles ahead of me, I won't see him. Maybe Rick will take care of him.

I usually ride behind David Lovejoy on these trips. David likes to ride Harleys too. I've seen him ride a Sportster for more than a thousand miles. I have to give him credit — he must have an iron butt. That bike was not meant for long distance. That's the kind of bike meant for riding from bar to bar. You know the bike I mean — the one everyone stands around and stares at the chrome. But, no one really wants to ride it all that far. It's too uncomfortable. Now, when you ride with David you have to be prepared. David likes to stop and take photos. Believe me, he stops a lot. He might only ride a half- mile. Watch out! If he sees something interesting, he's going to pull over. So, I don't get too close to David. I hang back and watch closely, so as not to crash into him when he stops unexpectedly. David likes landscapes and animals. You won't see many people in David's photographs. Sometimes, I wonder what the psychologists would say about that — all photos without people.

I've ridden short distances in Maine with John Kimball before. John likes to hang back and take the rear. I think it's because he doesn't trust the guy in front of him riding his other bike — me. I don't blame him. If I had a $25,000 Harley all tricked out, I'd be nervous too. I'm just thankful that he's generous enough to allow me to ride one of his bikes. I really think John is getting soft in his old age — I wouldn't let me ride it. Hell, Rick won't even let me touch his bike!

CHAPTER 40

Maine Folk

I'm just free-styling — writing about anything that comes to mind. Last night as I was in bed trying to get to sleep, I had some thoughts. I have thoughts every night. They aren't dreams. I don't recall dreams all that much. It's the thoughts that come to me before sleep that I remember. I always seem to have ideas at night before sleep. They seem like they would make good stories at the time. But, as the next day progresses, they don't seem so great. Maybe, that's why people say, "sleep on it," before making a decision.

As I was tossing and turning, I tried to compare digging up old memories to a walk in the woods and some excavating with a shovel. I mean, in my thoughts I found myself walking through the piney Maine woods beneath the swaying trees that were bending and creaking in the wind. I was walking on a bed of leaves and pine needles that had accumulated over hundreds of years — like behind my grandmother's home on Highland Avenue near the high school. In my thoughts, I was carrying a spade and walking on the soft forest floor until I came to an opening in the trees where the ground was even softer — like that above a grave. In my thoughts, I began digging the ground until I uncovered a steel door hidden by all the sod and debris. I sat and looked at the hole and the door. I then asked myself, "Why am I going to uncover this? Why bother to dig it up? I already know what's down there. Why bother to unearth something that is unpleasant and ugly?" I mean, what's the point? I already know that if I open that door, it's going to be scary. If I pull that stuff out of the ground, it's going to stink. It's going to be ugly and turn people off, as well as make me feel unpleasant. Isn't that why we bury things — so we don't have to see them? Some things just need to be covered. Because, if we don't cover them, they just stink up the place and turn people away.

Otherwise, we'd just let things lie above ground for everyone to see. I think it's better to let some things stay underground. Think about it. Once you've uncovered something distasteful, you can't just put it back. It doesn't work that way. The visual and the stench hang around forever.

Last night I got thinking about "drama." I'll have to admit, that lately I've tried to avoid drama. Yet, we all have friends who have drama. If we didn't, we wouldn't have any friends. You know what I mean? What's the point in being a friend, if we can't share the other person's drama? Isn't that what friendship is all about? I know it's not like I can do anything about someone else's drama. But, I can at least share it with them, or maybe listen to them share it with someone — someone like me. I guess that's what I never got right about my relationships with women. Take my girls for example. They would always share their drama. But, rather than just try to listen, I was always looking for solutions. I felt that I needed to solve their problems — end their drama — when all they really wanted was for me to listen. I guess that's what I missed. I couldn't just listen. I always felt that I needed to take action. Maybe that's why some people go to confession. I'm not a religious person. So, I'm only spit balling here. But, it seems to me that sometimes people just want someone to listen. So, they talk to someone who they don't really know hidden behind a screen of sorts. They talk to someone who doesn't try to solve their problems — someone who gives them some action that they need to take to resolve them. I guess it helps them feel better. Most men I know won't share their drama. Maybe that's why they eventually explode in anger. We keep all that drama built up inside until it has nowhere else to go but out in a burst of emotion. When that happens, watch out! You might eat a knuckle sandwich. Most women I know, on the other hand, are quick to release that pressure. We suffer though their drama for a short time. Then, once it's all out, they move on. It's amazing how they can do that.

I miss the people in Maine. When you ask someone from Maine how they are, be prepared for a real answer. They are going to tell you — they are going to share their drama. I remember my friend's mother. I knew her because she was our Den Mother when I was in Cub Scouts in South Portland back in the fifties. I would always try to see her when I went back to Maine on leave — back when she was still alive. Whenever I saw her, I would ask her how she was. Now, I knew that I needed to be sitting down, because her answer wasn't going to be the typical "fine," like I get these days in California. It wasn't, "I'm well; how are you?" It wasn't like the responses I get in Arizona or other places. When I asked Mrs. P how she was, I got an earful. That's what I wanted to hear — how things really were — who was not doing so well — who was drinking too much — who wasn't feeling well — that kind of stuff. That's what I miss about Maine. I don't get that response anywhere else. If you ask someone from Maine how they are, be prepared for the answer. It may take a while —you might need to sit down.

I miss the Maine old-folks. They knew how to live. Take my grandmother for example. She was poor but had everything. She had a house surrounded by woods — about eighteen acres of forested land in South Portland. She grew everything — strawberries, raspberries, blackberries and rhubarb. Wild blueberries grew on the rocky high ground behind her house. She had a home-made greenhouse where she grew all kinds of plants and flowers. There was a pond back in the woods loaded with pickerel, turtles and frogs. There were deer and bears and other wildlife in her woods. She spent hours watching the birds in the bird-feeders out back. I miss that life. That was back when two or maybe three generations of my relatives lived under one roof. There were uncles around, and my one-legged great-grandmother moved around the house on a stool rather than a wheelchair. I wish I had been there when Grammy lost the land. My grandmother was in her nineties when she tried to sell her land. She was blocked by the local politicians. They slow-rolled her with all kinds of excuses. Eventually, she ended up selling the land for a fraction of what it was worth to someone who was connected to city hall. They chopped the land up into lots and built a development with many homes. Someone else got rich off her misfortune.

I told you I was just free-styling. Maybe, I should just sleep on this stuff or get back to writing stories.

CHAPTER 41

Return from Italy

I basked in the memories of my trip to Italy. Darla from VanEvans Tours, LLC pulled out all the stops. It was VIP service from beginning to end. No details were left undone. She followed my every move from my house to the airport. She changed my flights when she found a better deal. She changed my seats when she thought she should. Her airline experience really made a difference. The accommodations she arranged were superb. We stayed in a waterfront villa near Bellagio on Lake Como. We had the best hotel on the Italian Riviera south of Genoa. We stayed in a Castle near Chianti. Our rooms in Cortona and Orvieto were within walking distance to their towns' center. We hiked the Cinque Terra. They guided us through the Galerleria dell' Accademia and the Galleria degli Uffizi in Florence. We had numerous tours of wine cellars and vineyards. Our accommodations in Rome were central and within walking distance to the train station. The meals throughout were to die for. The guides knew their stuff. They walked us through the Vatican and the Roman colosseum. It was one of my best trips. It was without a doubt the best travel package of my life.

I boarded the Southwest Airlines flight on my final leg home. I had an aisle seat. Darla knew my preferences. The couple next to me were a little younger than me. That's more common these days. They started a conversation. They were on their way to see their daughter graduate from the UCLA. They were excited. We started talking. Before I knew it, I was telling them about my trip. One thing led to another. We talked about our lives and our life experiences. I let them in on my life as a Marine and a pilot. We talked about my early days in Vietnam. We showed each other photos. Before I knew it, we were nearly back home in Orange County, California.

As I usually do these days, I excused myself to make a trip to the rest room before landing. When I returned to my seat, the pilot came on the intercom and told us it was time for us to prepare for landing. He gave us the weather in Irvine and thanked us for flying on Southwest Airlines. Then he said, "Since it's Memorial Day weekend, I'd like to take a moment and recognize one of our passengers. The passenger in seat 13C is a pilot and flew the President on Marine One. He was also a Vietnam veteran." I looked overhead and saw my seat number — 13C. As I did, the entire plane broke out in cheers and applause. I was stunned.

As I buckled my seat belt and raised my tray, I turned to the lady beside me and said, "I guess that will teach me not to leave my seat when I'm sitting next to you."

CHAPTER 42

Jason and Rob

"Strange, isn't it? Each man's life touches so many other lives, and when he isn't around he leaves an awful hole, doesn't he?" Those were the words of Clarence Odbody, the fictional angel who leapt from a bridge into an icy river for George Bailey to save in Frank Capra's 1946 film, *It's a Wonderful Life*. Like Clarence, providence placed Jason Maxwell in just the right place at the right time. It was a quirky twist of fate, with one man's life depending on — and entangled with — Jason's and the lives and decisions of so many others.

Seattle's sea-water temperature averages about fifty-four degrees Fahrenheit in August. On the 13th of August 2018, the water temperature was a frigid fifty-three degrees. Water that cold can bring on the effects of hypothermia in a matter of minutes. As hypothermia sets in, blood moves away from one's extremities toward their body's core. Ironically, people in good shape lose coordination and strength faster than those with an extra protective layer of insulating body fat. Jason Maxwell has very little fat on his 6'3" frame. A former US Army trained life guard, Jason was well aware of the hypothermia risk when he dove into Seattle's frigid water that day to save a crewmember who had fallen from a cargo ship and was drowning off Harbor Island.

Jason's father, Guy "Robbie" Maxwell, was my neighbor at Willard Beach in South Portland, Maine. He was also a good friend — we played together as kids. In 1969, as a nineteen-year-old Marine in Vietnam, Rob saved his platoon from an ambush and was later decorated for heroism. After his discharge from the Corps in 1970, he was out of work and looking for a job. I had just been discharged from the Army and was working as a surgical technician at Mercy hospital in Portland, Maine. When not at work, I spent a lot of time at Rob's parent's house. I was still dealing with the aftereffects of the war and felt comfortable there with someone who was also a Vietnam veteran. When I learned that Mercy needed another surgical tech, I recommended that Rob apply for the job. He applied, interviewed, and they hired him. I left Mercy a few months after Rob was hired — but not before becoming the best man at his wedding to Linda Hodgkins. I went to Memphis for college and later entered the Marine Corps. Unlike me, Rob was a perfect fit for the job at Mercy. The Doctors and staff loved him, and he worked in the operating room there for nearly thirty years. While I was gone, Rob became a personal assistant to Dr. Crane — one of the founders of the Orthopedic Associates of Portland. Rob and Dr. Crane were among the first to perform knee arthroscopy — initially, they practiced on cows' knees at a farm in Cumberland. Rob managed to turn a job that I sometimes hated into a career.

When I left Maine, I never went back — except to visit my family. My Marine Corps travels took me all over the states, and I eventually settled in Orange County, California. Sometime around 2001, while living in California, I received a call from Jason's brother, Tim. Tim told me of Rob's kidney cancer and asked if I would attend Rob and Linda's thirtieth wedding anniversary at the Snow Squall restaurant in South Portland — my appearance was to be a surprise for Rob, who I hadn't seen in nearly thirty years. It didn't take long to renew my friendship with Rob. After the wedding anniversary celebration, I made several trips back to Maine from California and spent time with Rob and his family. Rob was into four-wheeling at the time, and we had a blast riding along Maine's muddy roads and the fields and woods around Gray. Rob was always fun to be with — he had a wonderful personality and a great sense of humor. On one trip back to Maine, I went with him while he was shopping for a new suit. As he was getting fitted for his suit, the tailor asked him, "So, what's the occasion — a wedding?" Rob dryly answered, "No; I'm going to be buried in it." The tailor thought he was joking. I knew he wasn't. His cancer had advanced, and he had little time left.

The last time I saw Rob, I was at his home in South Portland. He routinely played cards with Linda and his extended family — his mother, brothers and sisters. After the card game, we talked a bit before I left for my sister's house. Rob — half joking and half serious — asked me to help find a job for Jason. I didn't promise anything, but I said that I would give it a try. Rob passed away on the 8th of June, 2004 from the effects of agent orange — another casualty of the Vietnam War. As chance would have it, shortly after his death, I learned of a job opening at the stevedoring company where I worked in Long Beach. It was an entry level management position, and I thought Jason would be a perfect fit — he was young, athletic, intelligent, and he had his dad's personality. People liked him — that's a big asset on the waterfront. About two years after Jason was hired and began working in California, I moved on. At nearly sixty years old, I knew my future in the stevedoring business was limited. It was a job for a younger person. Jason's career there was just beginning — mine was at an end. I took a desk job in Yuma, Arizona working with Marines again.

Fourteen years after leaving Maine for California, Jason was standing on a dock in Seattle, Washington. Jason had been promoted several times over the years, and was now the Vessel Operations Manager in charge of loading and unloading the many ships that brought their cargo to Terminal 18 on Harbor Island, Seattle. When Jason's cell phone rang, it was a manager from another terminal across the harbor on the line. Jason learned that there was someone in the water with his arms flailing about. Jason quickly looked for a life ring. Having found one, it was obvious that the person in the water was too far away from the dock — 100 to 150 feet. No one could hurl a life ring that far. Without hesitation, Jason kicked off his shoes and dove in the frigid water. As he swam, he lost sight of the man in the water — he had descended about ten feet below the surface. Fortunately, he had a bright orange uniform on which Jason was able to see as he dove under the waves. After grabbing the victim by the collar and pulling him up from below, Jason kept their heads above the sea water until a small watercraft happened by and helped pull both men from the water. Luckily, Jason had reached the crewmember in time to keep him from drowning. Except for the onset of hypothermia, both men were ok.

This incident got me thinking about life and how events are connected. There are a lot of "what if's" in this story. What if Rob and I hadn't both gone to Vietnam — would we still have been friends? If Tim hadn't called me — would I have seen Rob again — would we have renewed our friendship? What if Rob hadn't asked me to find a job for Jason? What if Jason hadn't taken the job — would someone else have been there to dive into the freezing water? There are so many questions — they can go on and on, indefinitely.

CHAPTER 43

The Wine Cellar

"He doesn't want to be that tall," Doctor Alvarez said. I took another look at the kid standing at the wine cellar bar. "How do you know that?" I asked. "Look — his knees are bent — he's slumped at the shoulders, and he's bent at the waist. He's trying to make himself the same height as his friends," he said. I looked again. Sure enough, I could see it. It was impossible to miss now. It got me thinking.

All my life, I've tried to be like those around me. I wore the same clothes. I had the same haircut — the same shoes. I had the same aspirations. I looked at my wine glass. I was drinking the same wine. I drank what they said was good. I didn't even taste it first. I just thought it must be good. It had to be. They told me it was good.

I don't talk to Doc Alvarez anymore. He makes me think too much.

I like going to the Old Town Wine Cellar in Yuma. Besides being a cool place in the summer, I get to see a lot of people I like in the winter. I also get to learn about wine. I'll have to admit, I've been trying to learn about wine for the last ten years. It's a difficult subject. But, I figure that there's no better place to learn about wine than in the Wine Cellar. It's not just that I'm surrounded by hundreds of bottles of wine. I'm surrounded by a lot of people who drink and like wine. I've tried to listen and pick up on their conversations. I have to admit, it can be confusing at times.

Mikey Schelhammer knows a lot about wine — he has to know — that's his job — he owns the place. I try to pick up bits and pieces of information — tidbits — that I can learn from Mikey. It's hard, though. Sometimes, Mikey talks about his wines as though they were people. I guess you get close to your wines when you own them. He talks about their "nose" and their "body." He throws around terms like "bold, fat, and tired." To be honest, I don't get it. I don't see any of those things. I guess that's why Mikey says that his wines are "complex." Everyone else seems to understand — I'm still learning. I watched Greg Myers hold his glass up to the light and say, "Yes, it has nice long legs." I didn't see anything except a streaky glass.

Sometimes, Mikey will show me the corks. I really don't know what I'm looking for. But, I nod my head and say, "Nice." He seems to be satisfied with that. I've noticed that he only does that with the red wines. I tried it once with a chardonnay. All I got was a strange look from Mikey. I showed Mikey my screw top once and I got another strange look. Apparently, people want good corks in their wine bottles. They must. The waiters are always showing me the corks when I go to a restaurant with Pav. What I don't understand is why they only pour me a little glass of wine. They always stand and watch me drink it. When I pay for a whole bottle, I'd like a full glass. What's the point of buying a bottle if they only pour me a few tablespoons of wine? I've got to the point now where I just say, "Nice cork; may I have a full glass, please." Again, I get the strange looks.

I like it when Mike Donovan comes in the wine cellar. Now, there's something special going on when Mike enters that I still haven't figured out. Everyone seems really excited. It's strange, though. He always sits in the same spot on the left side of the bar against the wall. I think it has something to do with him being a criminal lawyer. He must like that spot because he can see both entrances from there. He might be worried that some disgruntled client will come through the door looking for him. No one can sneak up behind him with his back against the wall. That's a good place to sit if you think you might soon be in a gunfight. Yes, a gunfight. You never know who's packing in Arizona. Trust me, there are as many guns in the restaurants and bars as there are in the local gun stores. Mike must be packing, 'cause they always show him respect. It's as if he was one of those guys on the Sopranos. They always make a big show about dumping his wine in some big glass container — they never do that with my wine. I asked Mikey Schelhammer about that without trying to sound too stupid. He said something about having to "let it breathe." See! There he goes with the body references again! My wine must be dead — I never get the big container.

I get nervous when Doctor Alvarez is at the Wine Cellar. He's a pathologist and the town's Coroner. I don't know if he's expecting something bad to happen to Mike Donovan or not. With all those guns in Yuma, I guess it's a good thing to have an MD around. You never know what might happen. Doctor Alvarez also knows a lot about wine. In fact, he owns his own winery in El Dorado, California. It's called the "Miraflores" winery. I've never been there, but I'm told it's a really nice place. I guess his wines must be pretty good. He said something about how they were graded 93 and above. That must be a really good grade. When I was in High School in South Portland, a 93 was an A. So, his wines must be really "bright." I heard Mikey say that about his wines once. See what I mean about how he uses that reference to people? I can't imagine how Doctor Alvarez can hold all those jobs. Hell, his winery isn't even in the same state. I had trouble holding one job — let alone jobs in different states. Doc Alvarez is a very smart guy, though. If anyone can figure out how to do it, he can. He's so smart that he scares me sometimes. He can read people real fast. He knows what they are thinking before they do. It makes me nervous. I don't like it when someone can read my mind. There's a lot of stuff going on in there that I don't want advertised.

Sometimes, the wine cellar can get real busy — like on the first Wednesday of the month. That's the night when ladies have their "networking" meetings. You know, what's strange? I've noticed that a lot of men show up for those meetings. Maybe they misunderstand. Thursday and Friday nights can also get busy. Mikey usually needs help behind the counter on those nights. Some of his customers help behind the bar. He must have some special agreement with Sergeant Major Ray Farley and "Corrugated" Mike. I see them behind the bar a lot. I don't think they get paid for their services. I think they get some special deal on Mikey's wines. Everyone seems to have a special deal but me. That's ok. I'm still learning.

Greg Myers fills in behind the counter whenever Mikey goes on vacation. Greg owns a lot of chickens. If you like chicken eggs, it's convenient to stop at the Wine Cellar and get your wine while ordering eggs from Greg Myers. I've learned a lot about chickens talking to Greg. Did you know that chickens lay an egg every day? I didn't. You can learn a lot hanging out at the wine cellar. It won't be long before I'm helping behind the bar. I can feel it.

CHAPTER 44

More Wine Cellar Satire

I met with Mikey Shelhamer last Wednesday evening to discuss my future at the wine cellar. I'm trying to work my way up — I want to work behind the bar like Ray Farley. Mikey said that of all the customers he's ever considered letting behind the bar — I was one of them. He said that I was doing pretty damn good for someone who knows absolutely nothing. He also said I was a natural leader — the other guys would follow me around just to see what I would do next. I'm excited. I asked him how I could continue to improve — I eventually want to be like Mike Donovan — he doesn't have to do anything. Donovan attracts all the women when he goes to the cellar. Now, don't get me wrong — I'm happily married — have been for 45 years. But, I'd like to have some of the attention that Donovan gets without the groveling I have to do at home. I'm not sure what I'd do with it. But, I'll cross that bridge when I get to it — if I ever do.

Mikey said if I was really serious, I should buy my wine from the other end of the wine cellar. I'm not sure what difference it makes. I've gotten pretty used to those wines on the bargain wall. It takes me a while to pick one out, though. I've noticed that Mikey keeps changing them and marking them down. I usually wait until the price has dropped three or four times before I select one. I'm not like Donovan — he's not very choosey selecting his wines. He always goes to the same tiny corner by the front door. It must get boring — there are only three or four selections there. I don't want to get stuck in that rut. I like a little variety. That's why I go to the bargain wall — the wines there are rare — after a while, they disappear — never to be seen again. I think Donovan will eventually get tired of drinking the same old stuff. I don't think he's even aware where the bargains are kept. I've never even seen him look there. If he was smart, he could cut his wine bill by half or more just by shopping around a little.

I have a few suggestions for Mikey on how to attract more customers. I think a big screen TV would help a lot. Customers could watch football and other sports while drinking. He might want to add a few attractive waitresses too. They would attract more men and make sure we always have enough beer nuts. All Mikey serves now are some stale crackers. He might want to consider having a Karaoke night. I've noticed that a lot of winter visitors like karaoke. The place needs more winter visitors. I haven't told him — but I think he needs to get rid of that dishwasher behind the counter. I don't think it's working all that well. Customers are always tasting things in their wine glasses — like oak, butter, fruits, and spices. I heard one customer complain that he tasted pepper. That dishwasher would be the first thing to go if I were in charge. If he had a deep sink, his helpers could wash and rinse the glasses behind the bar like they do at the Pint House. I think Mikey is wasting a lot of space too. He should stand his wines up like they do at the variety stores. He could fit twice as many bottles in his racks if he just stood them on end. Another thing — turn off that air conditioner at night. He keeps that thing running constantly — it's such a waste! Oh ya, I noticed Mikey keeps a spittoon on the bar. That can't be all that sanitary. If the board of health sees me spitting in that spittoon, they are likely to shut down the place. Just put it on the floor where it belongs.

Yup, I've got all kinds of ideas how to improve the place. I'll bring them up at our next meeting. Mikey said to let him know well in advance before we discuss my future again. I can't wait!

The End

About the Author

David S. Libbey is a displaced "Maine-iac" — a native of South Portland, Maine. He left Maine in 1968 after volunteering for the draft. David served as an enlisted man in the US Army for two years before attending college at Memphis State University. After graduation, David attended Officer Candidate School and was commissioned in the Marine Corps. He is a Vietnam Veteran and a retired helicopter pilot. David was a Presidential Aircraft Commander for President Ronald Reagan from 1984 – 1987. Before retiring from the Marine Corps, David commanded a Marine helicopter training squadron at Marine Corps Air Station, Tustin, California. After retiring as a lieutenant colonel, David worked in several jobs, including as a contractor for Science Applications International Corporation at Marine Aviation Weapons and Tactics Squadron One in Yuma, Arizona. Colonel Libbey holds a Masters in Management from Webster University. He currently resides in Trabuco Canyon, California.

Made in the USA
Monee, IL
01 November 2019